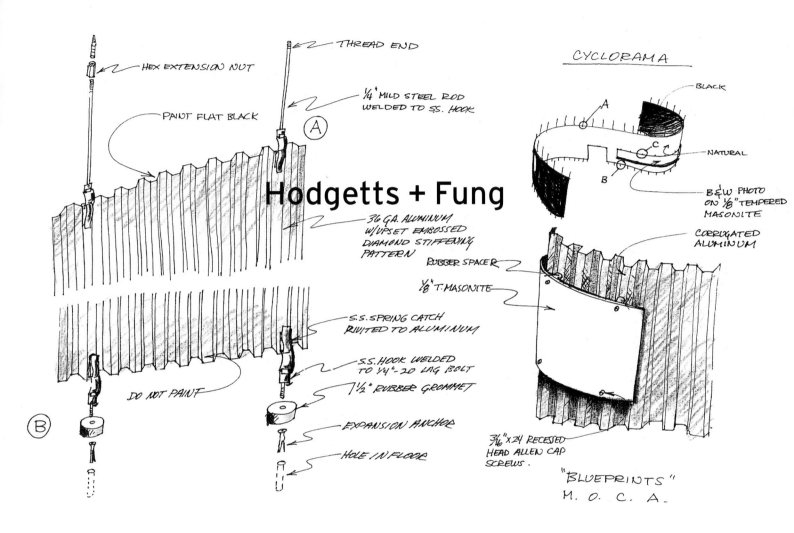

HEX EXTENSION NUT

THREAD END

PAINT FLAT BLACK

¼" MILD STEEL ROD
WELDED TO S.S. HOOK

(A)

CYCLORAMA

BLACK

A

C

B

NATURAL

B & W PHOTO
ON ⅛" TEMPERED
MASONITE

Hodgetts + Fung

36 GA. ALUMINUM
W/UPSET EMBOSSED
DIAMOND STIFFENING
PATTERN

CORRUGATED
ALUMINUM

RUBBER SPACER

⅛" T. MASONITE

S.S. SPRING CATCH
RIVITED TO ALUMINUM

S.S. HOOK WELDED
TO ¼"-20 LAG BOLT

1½" RUBBER GROMMET

DO NOT PAINT

(B)

EXPANSION ANCHOR

HOLE IN FLOOR

3/16" × 24 RECESSED
HEAD ALLEN CAP
SCREWS.

"BLUEPRINTS"
M. O. C. A.

Hodgetts + Fung

SCENARIOS AND SPACES

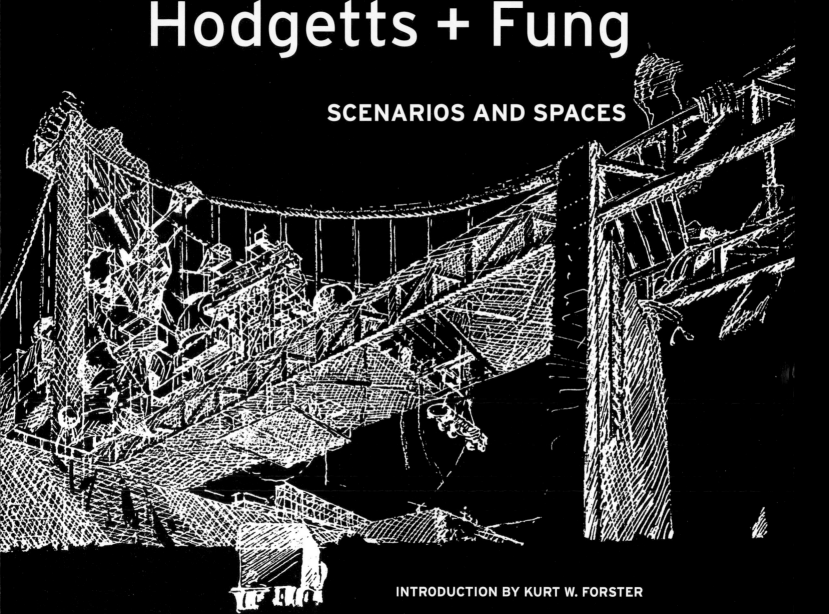

INTRODUCTION BY KURT W. FORSTER

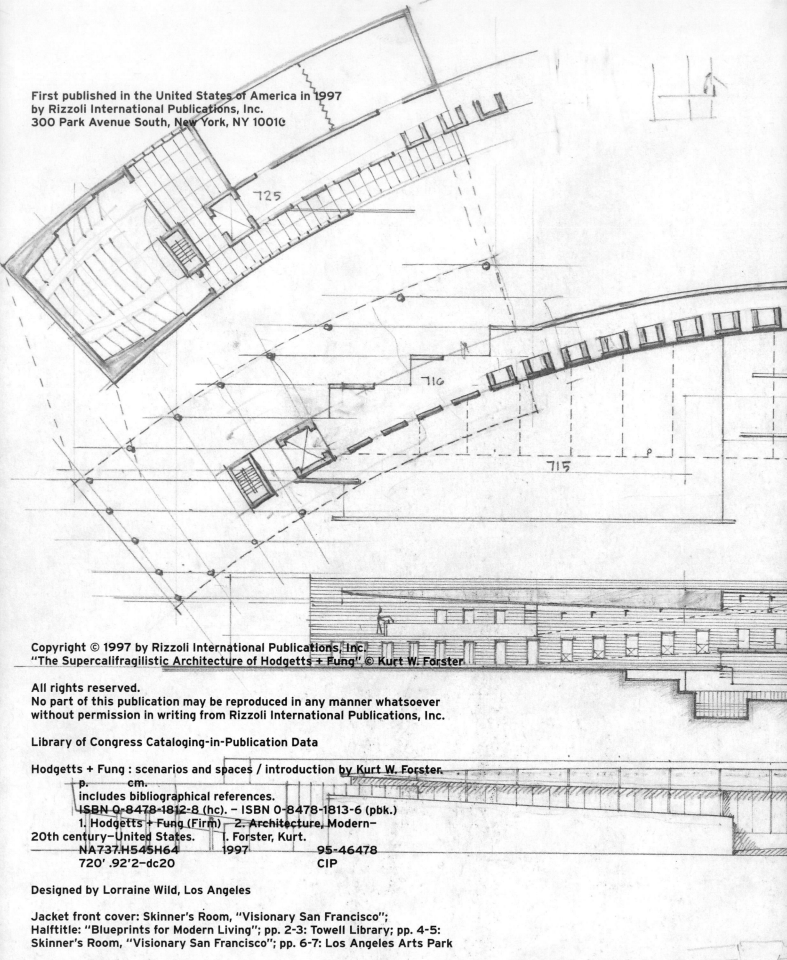

First published in the United States of America in 1997
by Rizzoli International Publications, Inc.
300 Park Avenue South, New York, NY 10010

Library of Congress Cataloging-in-Publication Data

Hodgetts + Fung : scenarios and spaces / introduction by Kurt W. Forster.
   p.   cm.
   includes bibliographical references.
   ISBN 0-8478-1812-8 (hc). – ISBN 0-8478-1813-6 (pbk.)
    1. Hodgetts + Fung (Firm)   2. Architecture, Modern–
20th century–United States.   I. Forster, Kurt.
   NA737.H545H64   1997   95-46478
   720' .92'2–dc20   CIP

Designed by Lorraine Wild, Los Angeles

Jacket front cover: Skinner's Room, "Visionary San Francisco";
Halftitle: "Blueprints for Modern Living"; pp. 2-3: Towell Library; pp. 4-5:
Skinner's Room, "Visionary San Francisco"; pp. 6-7: Los Angeles Arts Park

Printed and bound in Hong Kong

Preface

The evolution of our studio reflects the intelligence and commitment of the many extraordinary individuals with whom we have collaborated to achieve a common vision. Looking back, rather than aggressively ahead, has made us all the more aware of the privileged spot our studio has occupied, and of the versatility of those who helped to define it.

Thus the work gathered in this book rightly includes projects from Studio Works that precede our partnership and which we believe contribute to an understanding of our purpose and philosophy.

The first incarnation of Studio Works, on Union Square in New York, evolved from the short-lived office of James Stirling and Arthur Baker to become first the practice of Lester Walker and Craig Hodgetts, then a collaboration between Walker, Hodgetts, graphic designer Keith Godard, and Robert Mangurian of California. The multimedia shop they designed for Creative Playthings, together with a series of articles they published in Glamour, New York, and the newly formed Ms. magazines, established the tenor of our practice.

When Hodgetts and Godard relocated to California, Eugene Kupper and Peter de Bretteville joined them to form a West Coast branch of the office, Works West, which advanced the cause of mobility and technology, most notably in de Bretteville's own steel and glass house and in their design for a mobile theater.

A series of designs for feature film projects with production designer Brian Eatwell and writer-producer Zalman King helped to focus the studio on new ways of seeing and introduced us to the concept of storyboards as a design tool. At that time, Martin and Mickey Friedman commissioned a series of exhibitions and publications at the Walker Art Center in Minneapolis that allowed us to use these tools in an urban design context for the exhibition "The River: Images of the Mississippi."

Studio Works' first major commission, the Southside Settlement Community Center in Columbus, Ohio, came about as the result of the client seeing an earlier project, a daycare center designed by Mangurian in New York. After an initial parti lay dormant for lack of funding, Southside Settlement director Barbara Stovall encouraged patience while Hodgetts and Mangurian redesigned the project in Los Angeles.

That project, and a subsequent gallery for arts entrepreneur Larry Gagosian, formed the cornerstone of a practice in which Mangurian's unwavering principles of construction integrity and cultural resonance provided a welcome bulwark against the rise of postmodern fashion. The inclusion of the Southside Settlement as the first project in this book thus signifies our considerable debt to Robert and our mutual admiration for his continuing contributions to architectural education as Director of Graduate Studies at the Southern California Institute of Architecture (Sci-Arc).

In 1984, Ming returned from a trip abroad and invited Craig to collaborate on a limited competition, thereby establishing the working relationship that would become Hodgetts + Fung.

The Museum of Contemporary Art in Los Angeles was Hodgetts + Fung's first client. Julie Lazar, the curator of performance art, provided an opportunity for us to collaborate on a performance piece for the inaugural exhibition at the Temporary Contemporary, and Sherri Geldin, the museum's visionary associate director, invited us to take part in a limited urban design competition. Later, the museum's commitment to architecture and design, together with director Richard Koshalek's passion for architecture, led to our installation of "Blueprints for Modern Living: History and Legacy of the Case Study Houses." This major exhibition offered us the official support that meant so much to our fledgling practice.

Julie and Roger Corman, true to their reputation, then took a chance by inviting us to build the house in which they still live, and they invested the whole enterprise with their particular vision and enthusiasm.

Still, without the courage of Duke Oakley, Campus Architect for UCLA, our work may never have found a place on an institutional scale. He and Richard Weinstein, former Dean of the School of Architecture and Urban Planning, persuaded the university to trust our office with the creation of the new campus Gateway, and, later, of Towell Library, where for the first time we had the opportunity to implement many of the founding principles of our practice.

Former NEA program head Michael Pittas, who helped fund Works West studies for the Venice Interarts Center, has remained a friend and collaborator—most recently on a project for a nonprofit cinema group, The American Cinematheque, for which we are adapting the historic Egyptian Theater in Hollywood to state-of-the-art specifications.

Throughout the years we have been fortunate to have found the critical support so necessary to one's sense of meaning—at first from writers Joseph Giovannini and Paola Antonelli, and now through the wit and genius of Kurt Forster, who not only contributed the introduction to this book, but has been a confederate and friend since his arrival in Santa Monica in 1983 as founding director of the

Getty Center for the History of Art and the Humanities. Herbert Muschamp passionately defined the meaning of our work (and that of fellow Los Angelinos) for an East Coast unfamiliar with many of our premises. Thanks also to Paolo Polledri for arranging our collaboration with William Gibson during the gestation of his novel Virtual Light. We are grateful to Toshio Nakamura, the genial former publisher of a+u in Japan, for being able to articulate the many facets of our practice from a distance of nearly ten thousand miles.

We must also thank Aaron Betsky for helping to shape not only this book, but our office as well. We are grateful for the support he has extended the office—first as an architectural critic-at-large and now as Curator of Architecture and Design at the San Francisco Museum of Modern Art.

This book celebrates the many young architects and designers who have invested their passion and intelligence in helping to carry our projects forward. They have carried concepts to completion with the same commitment with which they have endured the frustration of delayed and stillborn ideas, only to return to the drawing board, ready to devote their energies to still another dream. John Casbarian, Thane Roberts, Frank Lupo, Audrey Matlock, Kevin Daley, Frank Clemente, John Trautmann, Robert Flock, and Lynn Batsch are among those who have left a considerable mark, helping to make our workplace hum like a Ferrari, and we thank them for it.

Finally, we must express our deep appreciation to the great modern masters who have supported and inspired our work. James Stirling was a professor, employer, friend, and mentor whose spirit continues to inhabit every design; while day after day we depend on the creative energy of Frank Gehry, a friend, formal beacon, and uncompromising guide.

Craig Hodgetts
Hsin-Ming Fung
June 1996

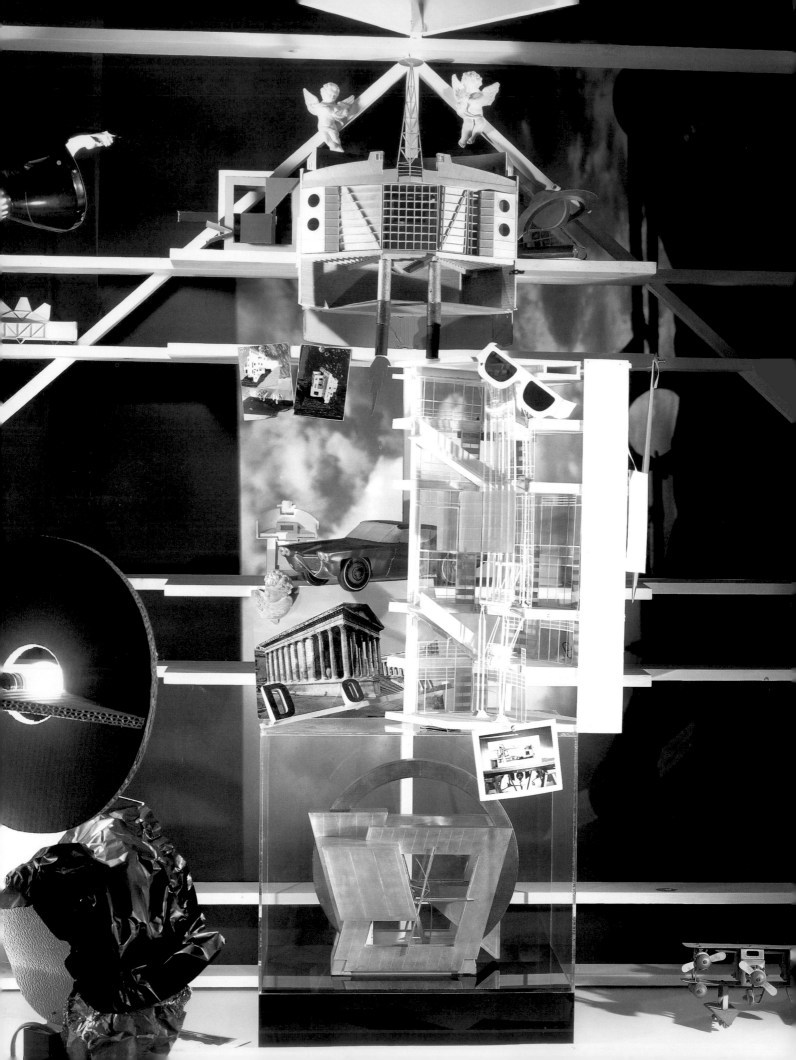

KURT W. FORSTER

The Supercalifragilistic Architecture of Hodgetts + Fung

Superficially, the works of Craig Hodgetts and Ming Fung may appear to belong to the sort of buildings that are qualified as ad hoc, ephemeral, and hybrid. These characterizations are partially true, but only narrowly so. Hodgetts + Fung manage to make real architecture rather than merely practical sense out of commissions of an incidental kind. In these instances, improvisation may be their strategy, but invention is their goal. On the other hand, it is no exaggeration to say that even their carefully planned and solidly built projects evince an air of impromptu festivity and uncertain fate. Their designs tend either to dissolve silently into the vernacular context from which they have been borrowed at will, or to clamorously spring from their surroundings like tents that may be pulled down at a moment's notice.

It lies in the nature of such constructions that they startle when they appear and never fully vanish from the mind. Bursting into view like a strip of celluloid images, they flash through our experience in the manner of cinematic episodes. Many of Hodgetts + Fung's drawings momentarily fix our eyes on a ledge, pull us under a footbridge, or suspend us in midair, without so much as a word of introduction. Hodgetts + Fung illustrate their tinkering in exploded views, putting screws and flanges in place as if they were rigging poetic machines for another age—an era that retains only the vaguest memory of machines as workhorses and transforms them into outlandish gizmos. In other drawings, the architects guide imaginary visitors through a building site in storyboard sequence, ransacking commercial stockpiles in search of a kit of useful parts. Useful, that is, to purposes far removed from those for which they were originally intended. Hodgetts + Fung are virtuosi of such improvised technology, as if they lived permanently in a postmechanical age in which all hardware has been converted into the endearing spoils of archaeology. Their best results, however, go beyond clever reuse and cunning adaptation and assume montage to be the operative technique of design.

Conference room,
Hodgetts + Fung
Design Associates,
Santa Monica, California

California has always had its share of cultural prophets and doomsayers. Railroad barons, aerospace industrialists, pioneers in everything from back-to-basics to seismology, and of late, the wizards of the virtually real life of the media have rarely been able to resist its temptations. Hollywood counts as the biggest of their many successes, for its industry of illusion best fulfills the promise of California's capacity to create something out of nothing. The mentality of cinematic production has made inroads into California culture far beyond the reach of the medium itself. Hodgetts + Fung's affinity for certain manufacturing techniques, and their numerous proposals to adapt and insert fabrication processes into housing schemes, shop displays, and furniture making, extend a set designer's disposition to the realm of daily life. Their architectural design increasingly assumes tasks that previously had been left in the hands of craftspeople or reserved for amateurs and dilettantes: the production of settings for practical rather than exclusively theatrical life.[1]

A further consequence of California's propensity toward blurring distinctions between the necessary and the illusory, the anonymous and the intimate, is a certain stylish irreality of life itself. Just as the irreality of films is more compelling than a steady stream of propositions for unorthodox living (and dying), and even more stimulating than the warning labels with which Californians lobby to bar toxic, noxious, and nihilistic threats from the public domain, so it has fallen to architecture to transform the given into the found, the elementary into the hybrid. Instead of resting on historic foundations, Californians like to project their imagination beyond the present into a wishful realm of possibilities. They are ever tempted to dabble in historic speculation or technological fantasy. The latter has proven even more irresistible than the endless retelling (and retailing) of the former, because conjecture has a stronger hold on our imagination than the past. Cinematic fantasies, in synchrony with the technical properties of film, lend a metaphorical validity to this predilection for calculated irreality.

Fragile as an aura, films have a curious presence in this culture: either they are in the process of being made or they are leaving their impressions (and, as fear would have it, wreaking psychological havoc) on the viewer, but otherwise they are virtually intangible. The images of a movie are entirely exterior to their material carrier, for we do not experience film in the way we reckon with paint, clay, or metal in our experience of traditional artifacts. Cinematic images are not made <u>of</u> film, but merely recorded <u>on</u> it. The nature of the medium resides in its projection for the viewer, and, though the life of the cinematic image appears to be immaterial, this fugitive effect is also its only substance. In contrast to the classic arts, but with an affinity to architecture, films are the epitome of post-modern production and consumption in one other respect: they result from an extremely complex (and often non-hierarchical) labor process and depend on the patronage of large communities of viewers. In their extreme diffuseness, films exercise an almost mythic effect with no clear cultural contours.

Cinema aesthetics thus are not only contaminated by the mechanisms of production and reception, but are limited to the one aesthetic of contamination. Its 'impurity' has long been the principal argument against ranking cinema among the arts at all. It is, however, precisely film's contaminated aesthetic that secures acceptance and causes lasting and widespread enjoyment of one of the fundamental methods of modern art-making. This method resides in the manipulation of bits and pieces of debris from everyday life. By salvaging snippets from the dregs, artists delve into the stuff of life for the making of art. Collage and montage not only recall their origin in the gutter, but also produce sublimated mementos. As Ernst Bloch argued in the 1930s, collage represents a key experience of modernity itself.[2] In its lack of stability, or, more accurately, in its fragility, montage acknowledges the ruinous state of its material while indulging in the irrationality of its own creation.

John Haberle (1856-1933).
Chinese Firecrackers, n.d.
Oil on canvas.

Generically, collage (and, by extension, assemblage and montage) finds a surprisingly independent ancestry in a particular category of American still-life painting generally known as trompe l'oeil. This art was practiced beyond the legitimizing aesthetic boundaries of its time by a peculiar group of largely self-taught painters, such as William M. Harnett, John Frederick Peto, Charles Meurer, John Haberle, and others.[3] Such trompe l'oeil painting—far from merely fooling the eye as its name might suggest—operates at the threshold between the physical world and its image. The painter substitutes images for the presence of things by means of illusion, or, in a word, by faking them. No accident, then, that graphically accurate representations of dollar bills, newspaper clippings, and imitation textures (long before they became the chief ingredients of cubist collages in the early years of the twentieth century) were the aesthetic proving ground among the ranks of trompe l'oeil painters. Of objects that were themselves already reproductions—chromolithographs, theater tickets, labels, and photographic images—these painters produced simulacra. The vague absurdity of their exercises, far from redeeming itself, actually added to the aesthetic uncanniness of their images.

If I make a connection between the ideas of Hodgetts + Fung and turn-of-the-century trompe l'oeil painting, I imply no superficial resemblance, but rather a profound similarity of disposition toward the world. With one and the same gesture, Hodgetts + Fung acknowledge the construct of our civilization as in a state of ruin while extending a hand to salvage its debris in their act of assembling <u>another</u> architecture. Unavoidably made of heterogeneous things, their lovingly illicit compositions lend a material toughness to the delicacy of their montage.

Lists constitute a means of ordering heterogeneous things and those that have fallen into pieces. There is a particular enumerative aesthetic in American art, one that John Cage has practiced and imbued with a literalness suggested by his claim that the two subjects dearest to him, mushrooms and music, are simply adjacent entries on the pages of an encyclopedia. Collected according to an entirely extraneous system, the alphabet, and then collaged together, things or words become imbued with a new meaning, a meaning forged by their conjoining. When the painter Stuart Davis was asked what held special interest for him as an artist, he recited a most heterogeneous list of things.[4] The glue that holds such lists together, beyond the hollow regime of all lists, is a will to fasten things together for poetic ends. Wherever one looks in the work of Hodgetts + Fung, one is struck by just such deliberate montage. Deeply marked by the experience that nothing holds together any longer but what has been joined and bound together by artifice, the architects have turned some of their most ephemeral work into a veritable theater of montage.

With their design for the temporary Powell—or Towell—Library on the University of California campus at Los Angeles, Hodgetts + Fung have carried their principle of montage to the farthest extreme: Here, their modus operandi extends beyond the task of fitting the pre-existing site with new structures rigged from prefabricated parts.[5] The new parts, which compose the tent-and hangar-like buildings, are themselves but pieces of a larger assemblage. Far from allowing a general relaxation of standards, such temporary buildings actually depend on an extreme economy of materials and judicious fabrication processes. The

playful appearance of the multifarious complex belies the rigor of its program and the constant stresses to which it is exposed. Its presumably short lifespan is no measure of the ingenuity invested in its construction. A veritable array of inventive moves, the Towell Library shares with some of Hodgetts + Fung's exhibition installations the wizard's touch, a capacity to make from old and new, from the tried and true catalogue of available and custom parts, something that has the freshness and power of magic.

[1] An aspect of California architecture I have discussed in regard to the practice of Frank O. Gehry (e.g. in my essay "Improvisations on Locations," in The Architectural Review 182 [1987], p. 65f and elsewhere) and in "Beauty (and the Beast) in the Parlor: Hodgetts+Fung's Architecture in the (C)Age of Media Culture," in a+u 3 (1991), p. 72f.

[2] See Ernst Bloch, Erbschaft dieser Zeit (Zurich: Oprecht & Helbling, 1935). Recently translated by Neville and Stephen Plaice and published as Heritage of Our Times (Berkeley and Los Angeles: University of California Press, 1991).

[3] I have discussed the relevance of trompe l'ocil paintings to modern American art in "Abbild und Gegenstand: Amerikanische Stilleben des späten 19. Jahrhunderts," in Bilder aus der Neuen Welt, catalogue of the exhibition in Berlin and Zurich (Munich: Prestel Verlag, 1988), pp.100–07 (with literature and entries for individual paintings, nos. 68-79).

[4] The list includes, among other things, "...Civil War and skyscraper architecture; the brilliant colors of gasoline stations, chain-store fronts, and taxi-cabs; the music of Bach; synthetic chemistry; the poetry of Rimbaud; fast travel by train, auto, and aeroplane...; electric signs;...5 & 10 cent store kitchen utensils, movies and radio; Earl Hines' hot piano...," in Herschel B. Chipp, editor, Theories of Modern Art: A Source Book by Artists and Critics (Berkeley and Los Angeles: University of California Press, 1986), p. 524.

[5] cf. my essay "Panem et Circenses," in a+u 5 (1993), p. 28f. I wish to thank Nancy and Louis Kent for helpful hints regarding Mary Poppins, and, of course, Denise L. Bratton for her expeditious editorial care.

**SOUTHSIDE SETTLEMENT COMMUNITY CENTER,
COLUMBUS, OHIO, 1980**
DESIGN PARTNER: ROBERT MANGURIAN/STUDIO WORKS

Gritty Pomp :

The settlement's ideals of hard work and integrity, explored
in a participatory design process, led to a hard-headed approach

Toward a New Humanism

to sustainability in the design of this community building in a depressed
area of Columbus, Ohio. We hoped to elevate common materials
and a no-nonsense attitude toward finishes by invoking a geometric order
that confers a strong sense of personal space, thus imbuing users
with a secure image of themselves. We also hoped to demonstrate the value
of a design effort proportionate to need rather than budget.

The building envelope is an "overcoat" that blends with the shingles
prevalent in the neighborhood but also provides an insulation shield for
the thermal mass of the concrete-block walls, thus stabilizing interior
temperatures and conserving the settlement's always precarious funding.

```
THE DISCOVERY OF PLACE IN A TYPICAL AMERICAN STREETSCAPE REQUIRES
      SOME INGENUITY. HOW IS ONE NOT TO SPY THE INGENIOUS THING AT A DISTANCE
           DOWN THE UBIQUITOUS BREADTH OF ROUTE 66?
HOW ALSO TO MANIFEST "PLACE" IN A PRIVATIZED CONTEXT
      WHEREIN THE BLOCKS, THE FACING PROPERTIES, AND EVEN THE AIR
                  ARE AVAILABLE TO THE HIGHEST BIDDER?
```

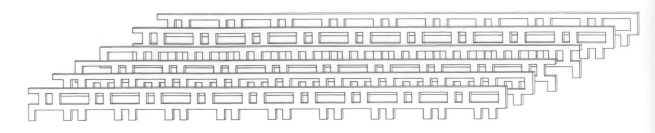

Other cost-saving innovations—formed troffers for lighting between exposed slabs of prestressed concrete and spiral-wound galvanized tubing used as formwork for columns—became briefly identified with the California Style and have long since passed into the vernacular, becoming prerequisites for hip shopping centers and houses.

The settlement is designed to be not so much a center as a presence in the neighborhood. The height of the principal cornice aligns with the "tin man" additions to the existing porches on the block. The gray concrete sheathing establishes a middle ground for the muddled pinks and greens of surrounding houses. The settlement hall on the corner replaces a house of similar mass.

In the ten years since construction the children who wait for a school bus at the site have adopted the entrance ramp and overlook as their own neighborhood castle. On a recent visit they implored the strangers (us!) not to tear it down.

SYMPATHY FOR CONTEXT IS
  BY NO MEANS AN AUTOMATIC RESPONSE.
WE HAVE ALL CONFRONTED SITUATIONS THAT
    REQUIRE DRAMATIC INTERVENTION, JUST AS
  WE HAVE DISCOVERED THOSE WHICH CALL FORTH
A PROFOUND REGARD FOR CONTINUITY.

The new building for the Southside Settlement is in a portion of Columbus known for its tenacious community spirit in spite of numbing poverty and systematic neglect. The architectural challenge was to represent the community values of self-reliance, determination, and realism that pervade the organization's activist polemic yet also to provide accommodation for the round-the-clock activities of a town center.

Our initial proposal attempted to translate those values directly to the construction process by means of a do-it-yourself structural matrix to be completed by the users. When this was rejected by the director, who pointedly reminded us that their politics were about issues more demanding than the position of a wall, our revised design premise emulated what "might have been" had the building come into being concurrently with the evolution of the Southside Settlement itself.

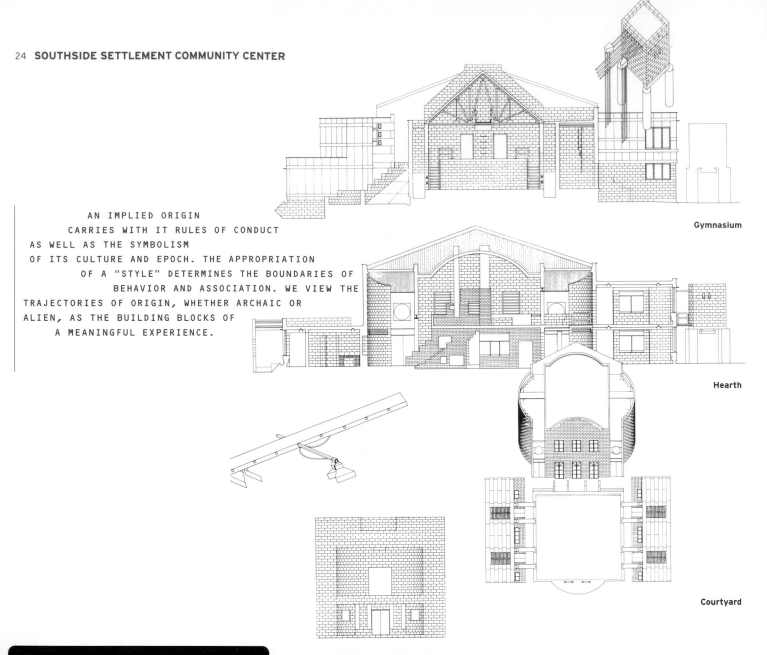

Gymnasium

AN IMPLIED ORIGIN
CARRIES WITH IT RULES OF CONDUCT
AS WELL AS THE SYMBOLISM
OF ITS CULTURE AND EPOCH. THE APPROPRIATION
OF A "STYLE" DETERMINES THE BOUNDARIES OF
BEHAVIOR AND ASSOCIATION. WE VIEW THE
TRAJECTORIES OF ORIGIN, WHETHER ARCHAIC OR
ALIEN, AS THE BUILDING BLOCKS OF
A MEANINGFUL EXPERIENCE.

Hearth

Courtyard

COMPETITION FOR ROOSEVELT ISLAND, NEW YORK, 1976

This housing competition for the City of New York envisioned a community of affordable housing on a neglected and underused island that once contained a notorious mental institution.

With fixed boundaries and an inviolate spatial surround, the island hardly seemed a candidate for the endless grids that characterize American cities (and dictate both their speculative economy and dispersed amenities) and even less a subject for traditional modernist housing. Our proposal views the island as "walled" city, accepting and exploiting the water's edge as well as the limited points of entry. A network of ceremonial public spaces graphically similar to an electronic circuit (itself remarkably similar to Nolli's analysis of public and private space) defines residual accommodation for housing.

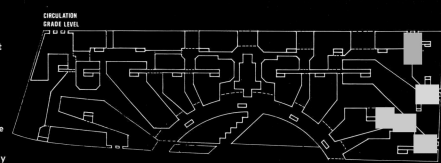

CIRCULATION
GRADE LEVEL

As in Southside Settlement, the dominant public realm and the rejection of geometric order would lead, we hoped, to a genuinely individual configuration for each apartment unit, in a matrix suffused by everyday amenities.

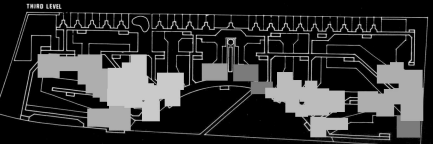

THIRD LEVEL

Accordingly, the building is conceived as a village, drawing on the figure-ground relationships of medieval townscapes. Interior spaces are defined by spatially "positive" outdoor rooms of the sort encountered in Venice or Florence, which very often result from accretive growth. Enclosing walls then evoke the inhabitants' individual identities.

Ceremonial devices, like the paired spiral columns supporting over-scaled portals, ennoble the individual user and refer to the scale, proportion, and grandeur of a courtyard such as that of the ducal palace in Venice.

Twentieth-century stagecraft exploits symmetry as a "neutral" background for the spontaneous asymmetry of human interaction;

focus is thus directed to the occupants rather than to an abstract architectural space.

When Southside's director reacted negatively to our first design essay, the appropriateness of this theory became clear. Like the Free Speech movement that formed in Berkeley in the sixties, the Settlement sympathizes with the vernacular over the corporate and tolerates differences as opposed to imposing uniformity. The "imperfections" of the occupants as well as those of the construction process were not only acceptable but polemically important. The incongruity of labor-intensive craftsmanship in a working-class neighborhood was to be replaced by an appropriate and durable palette that reflected simple construction.

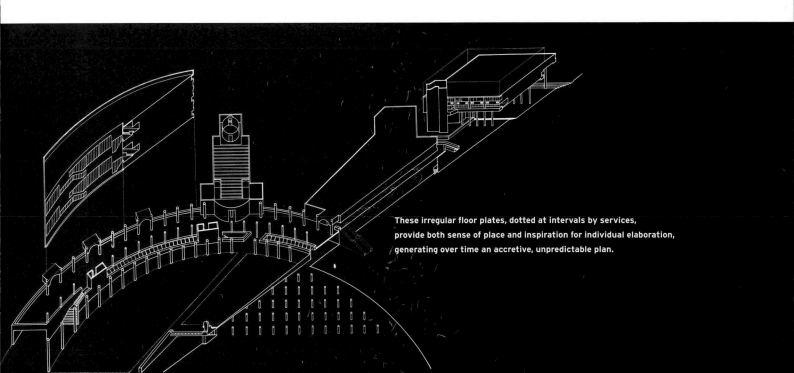

These irregular floor plates, dotted at intervals by services, provide both sense of place and inspiration for individual elaboration, generating over time an accretive, unpredictable plan.

HUDSON WILCOX MIXED-USE DEVELOPMENT, HOLLYWOOD, CALIFORNIA, 1992

This multiuse center to be constructed over the Hollywood station of the new Los Angeles Metro suggests reciprocity between street grid and defined public space.

Concern for the continuity of Hollywood Boulevard determined the husk of open-air markets, a produce hall, and a truck dock that buffers the terraced housing and offices and modulates access to the gritty streetscape below.

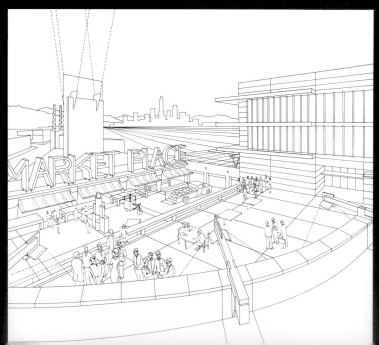

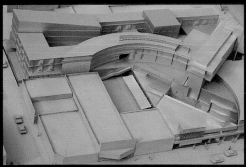

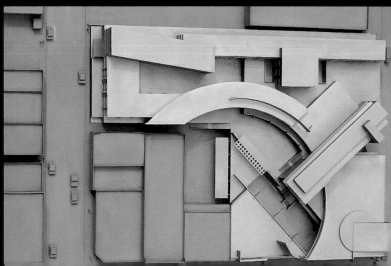

Los Angeles has a tradition of petite towers, dating from the thirties, in the Miracle Mile district. Eminently suitable for the agents, photographers, and leveraged hustlers who occupy the show-business fast lane, this tower emulates the emblematic towers of Siena or Modena within a modern vernacular.

Massing and construction of the Southside Settlement were strongly influenced by James Stirling's housing at Ham Common, in which the rich texture is derived from the compositional opportunities offered by different materials. Stirling's laboratories at the University of Leicester and his library at Cambridge University were powerfully on our minds for their adroit handling of the intersection between building masses; Alvar Aalto's early work at Sänyätsalo established a tone suitable to the modest surroundings and winter weather; Herman Hertzberger's student union in Amsterdam and later office complex in Apeldoorn, the Netherlands, demonstrated the formal possibilities inherent in concrete-block construction.

The narrative structure here occurs within the building's eclectic spatial and material vocabulary. Archetypal forms—rounded, angular, geometric, and interstitial—are arranged to provoke specific responses. Nonlinear readings of architectural spaces, as of CD-ROMs, offer innumerable event sequences. Scenarios of revision, remodeling, and even repair by other (imaginary) architects influenced the final design, much as they would in creating a fictitious setting for a play. A fascination with the European plaza, in which a palpable space is defined by a motley collection of surrounding structures, led us to challenge assumed unity.

We hoped to design a space that might be perceived as regular and rigorous while the graphic compositions of its defining forms suggest different, perhaps even dissonant emotions. We developed a "feminine," rather sympathetic and symmetrical central building; a "masculine," dark, and dominant theater; and a civic, ceremonial flanking wall. The "place" is defined by the proximity of these dissimilarities and the resolution of their differences.

We prefer to think of architectural character in vernacular terms, where richness of experience is a function of a variety of "imaginary" authors working within a single vocabulary. The individual attributes of these building types are both amplified and muted by their adjacencies, suggesting the architectural equivalent of a congenial group, perhaps enjoying an after-dinner conversation—full of familiarity and faithful memories.

GAGOSIAN HOUSE AND GALLERY, VENICE, CALIFORNIA, 1979
STUDIO WORKS

Access to natural light and the owner's lifestyle as a latter-day don in present-day Venice, California, suggested the traditional palazzo as a model for the absolute division of public and private realms. A robust, even belligerent street presence armored in the skid plate and metal screens of Soho truck docks guards an interior configured by the justified axes and processions of its compromised site.

A LIMITED INVENTORY OF MATERIALS OFFERS THE
OPPORTUNITY TO ADDRESS THEMATIC VARIATIONS
OF ELEMENTS WITHIN A SYNTACTIC FRAMEWORK.
GIVEN THE ELEMENTAL NATURE OF
CONSTRUCTION MATERIALS,
SIMPLE EVENTS, SUCH AS THE ROTATION
OF A STRUCTURAL GRID,
ACQUIRE MEANING UNATTAINABLE WITH
A MONOLITHIC MATERIAL.

Within a central drum, a faux symmetry stabilizes a required setback,
an offset stair, and a mechanical intrusion. The figural stair and pulpit, like
the balcony in the Viso House, suggest habitation.

The second drum, smaller and packed with
equipment, provides a compact area for
food preparation and cooking, and offers a
figural counterpart to the spatial void of
the larger drum.

The hand of the laborer here is never disguised. The screws, mortar, battens, and metalwork bear the mark of human manufacture and assembly, which we felt was critical to a prominent building in a working-class neighborhood. At Southside we attempted to sustain this character through cabinetwork, handles, and railings that are there as much for the hand as for the eye.

The tension between the informal exterior of the street elevation and the formal exterior elevation of the courtyard was resolved through careful articulation of material. Off-the-shelf operable windows on the street elevation, custom wood windows on the "contained exterior space" (courtyard), and the same custom wood on the "contained interior" (gymnasium) exploit pronounced differences in scale and attitude toward finishes and materials.

In addition, the sober configuration of the concrete block itself—a shape so basic as to seem untouched by human intelligence—integrates with the realm of geometry, in which such a basic element makes complete sense. Simply to be "in fashion" seemed far too facile in this context. After all, this is a street with no "preferred elevation." The resulting structure offers few clues to the hierarchy of front and back. Both merge almost indistinguishably into the neighborhood. A "wallpaper" elevation offers a repetitive, textural experience rather than a graphic composition that establishes visual hierarchy.

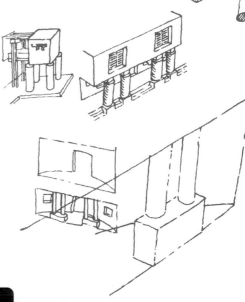

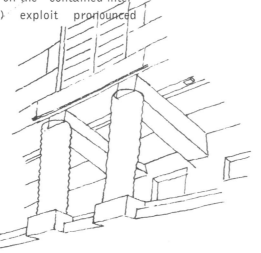

VISO HOUSE,
HOLLYWOOD, CALIFORNIA, 1990

There are a number of enduring prototypes for the Los Angeles hillside house. Most are stucco, framed simply with wood and modest spans, with volumes often dictated by the hand labor of digging on precipitous slopes (one thinks of Sperlonga, Siena, Urbino) since mechanized equipment often can't reach such sites. Typical planning is likewise often discarded due to peculiarities of land, views, and access, leading to topsy-turvy priorities, labyrinthine circulation, and often startling accommodation to terrain.

The design of this house began with the premise of a vertical cylinder and a surrounding cube arranged so that the cylinder would provide structure and act as the formal spline for a relaxed arrangement of intersecting volumes.

Visitors first view the interior from a tiny interior balcony overlooking the living space, before returning to the staircase. There they find crisscrossing access to the floors above and below.

THE COLLECTIVE GENIUS
OF THE BALLOON FRAME,
OF CORRUGATION, OF THE
RIGHT ANGLE, AND OF
THE CONCRETE BLOCK IS OURS
TO REVEAL.

The standard inventory of builder's materials provided the palette. The identity of each volume derives from the specific geometric protocol of its fenestration. Diluted color was applied using push brooms and ladders.

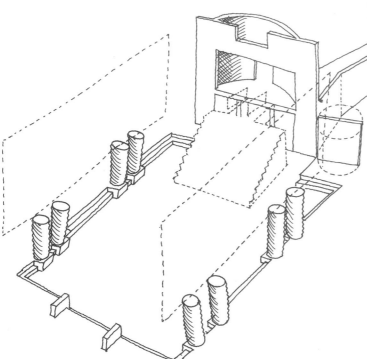

TOWELL LIBRARY, UNIVERSITY OF CALIFORNIA AT LOS ANGELES, 1992

The need to provide a compact yet distinctive transition from the extruded space of the Towell Library reading room to the hemicycle of the periodical space suggested a third, crimped volume that we call the "hammock." Students sleep and read there. It is also a portal whose axes and terminations, though executed in tissue-thin materials, direct the eye and body as effectively as masonry masses.

"BLUEPRINTS FOR MODERN LIVING," EXHIBITION DESIGN, THE MUSEUM OF CONTEMPORARY ART, LOS ANGELES, 1989

The environment of Frank Gehry's Temporary Contemporary provided a context for the black aluminum curtain and portal that begin the narrative for "Blueprints for Modern Living."

LOS ANGELES ARTS PARK, SEPULVEDA BASIN, LOS ANGELES, 1989

Our winning master plan for this center for the arts envisions a collection of buildings designed by different architects, each with a "front door" opening on a vast, circular promenade. The pervasive grid, recreating a typical San Fernando Valley orange grove, provides dramatic contrast to the flat-lathed disk of the central meadow. A radial axis extends views from a winged propyleaum on the circumference to a mountainous horizon to the south. Framing, uniting,  yet alien to each is the overhead structure of the Natural History Museum. It is a landscape designed to provoke curiosity and terminate certainty.

VENICE INTERARTS CENTER, VENICE, CALIFORNIA, PROJECT, 1983
STUDIO WORKS

A space to structure arts activities in spite of the rush of traffic and the memory of incarceration, this community arts center incorporates an existing jail and city hall. The geometry embraces the adjacent boulevard and median strip, carving an arc through the arched roof of the proposed library to create a progression of layered virtual spaces that unify the otherwise disparate elements and recenter the activities of the artists who meet and work there.

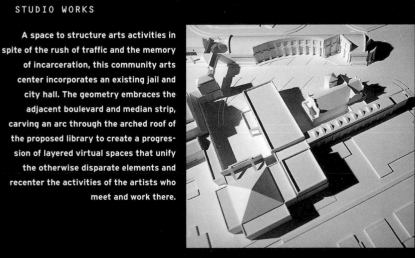

SEOUL SUMMER OLYMPICS ATHLETES' AND REPORTERS' VILLAGE, SEOUL, KOREA, 1985

The Korean dwelling typology mandated south-facing living spaces and established rigid guidelines that regulated building height and proximity. In this competition entry, we proposed a gigantic geometric order within which such rules exist "in context."

The horizontal datum established by an arc of aerial lookouts echoes the crescent form of the park below.

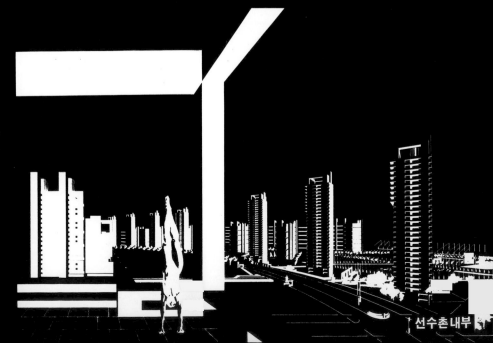

선수촌내부

RUINS SPEAK TRUTHFULLY
OF THE EFFECTS OF SCALE,
        PROPORTION, AND REGULARITY.
   SHORN OF INSTITUTIONALIZED MEANING,
    VALUABLE MATERIALS, AND
   ARISTOCRATIC HABITATION,
        SOME REMAINS NEVERTHELESS CALL FORTH
OUR HEARTFELT REVERENCE.

CRAFT AND FOLK ART MUSEUM, LOS ANGELES, 1995

Originally known as The Egg and the Eye, this Los Angeles arts institution finally assembled the resources to expand into a museum proper. Choosing to retain the identity of its original building, CAFAM acquired an adjacent vacant lot and neighboring structure with the intention of combining the ensemble into a single museum entity.

To join these two buildings, already distanced in space, time, and attitude, with a third element in order to form a practical whole suggested the creation of a nonbuilding that nevertheless catalyzes union. The orientation enables the sun to backlight the ensuing ramps and identity screens.

Visitors crossing from gallery to gallery have the opportunity to establish contact with those in the garden below, as well as to refresh their senses, before viewing the exhibitions in the adjacent building.

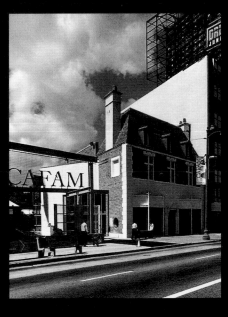

In the design of this forty-unit apartment
we sought to echo John Entenza's hope

Parts and Wholes:

for a housing prototype "capable of duplication and
in no sense an individual performance."

But where his concern was for the nuclear family of the American dream,
ours was for the fragmented heirs to the inner city; and where his objective
was to nurture the sublime resonance of aesthetics and technology,
ours was to expect the jangle of unforeseen events.

This housing, after all, is a response to those who brought their families,
their customs, and their lifestyles to Los Angeles, which is fast becoming
the most ethnically diverse city on the planet. Meanwhile
the city is on the brink of a cybernetic revolution.

Thus, we sought to redefine personal domain, lifestyle,
and technological opportunities for housing in a
realistic context. Flexibility was essential if the project was to
provide a prototype to be used and abused by merchant builders.

Therefore we deployed a set of simple elements
on the site for the purpose of demonstration.

The first is a private outdoor space adjacent to each unit that replaces
the largely symbolic public spaces of the typical apartment building.
The second is a system of paseos derived from California's Latin heritage,
which provides an address for each unit on its own miniaturized "street."
Third, a prefabricated technical core incorporating circulation, kitchen,
and bath, as well as optimized utilities, provides domestic services.

A GOOD COOK WILL SET OUT HIS/HER TOOLS IN GOOD ORDER
TO PERFORM WITH EFFICIENCY AND PREDICTABILITY.
SO IT IS WITH THE PRODUCTION LINE,
WHETHER OF CARS, HOUSES, OR FOOD.
THE NOTION THAT THE ESSENCE OF CRAFT IS LOST
IN SUCH A PROCESS IS NONSENSE.

The core element takes advantage of the structural redundancy of storage, stairways, and bathing compartments to produce an integrated monocoque structure of steel stampings at a substantial reduction in cost. Further savings are possible by adapting assembly processes from industry, such as the prefabricated looms used for electrical wiring, and OEM-style equipment (which can be shipped and installed without traditional casework and packaging). Reduced energy consumption is anticipated through closed-cycle heating and cooling, which recirculate the lost energy of cooking, refrigeration, and hot water. We assigned specific functions to the prefabricated core and more generalized functions to a moderate-span adjacent space.

Construction on a given site may employ sticks and stucco, concrete block, or light metal framing, depending on configuration and market conditions. However, the long-span capabilities of the monocoque structure ease adaption to hilly terrain, automobile storage, and mom-and-pop stores on the ground floor.

Once installed, the neutral spaces, activated by a dense overlay of amenities, will encourage tenants to evolve their own living patterns. For many that may be no more than arranging the furniture, but for some it will mean creating a separate entrance for an office at home, abandoning separately defined rooms, or "annexing" outdoor areas with lightweight structures. As each occupant exercises this right, the fabric of the whole will be defined for all and by all.

THE INDUSTRIAL WORLD IS DOMINATED
BY A MODULAR ETHOS SO PERVASIVE THAT ARCHITECTS
MUST NOW SEEK RELIEF FROM THE DICTATES OF AN
INFLEXIBLE SYSTEM RATHER THAN IMPLORE SUPPLIERS
FOR A RATIONAL COMPONENT.

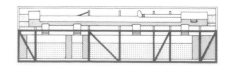

Core

Section

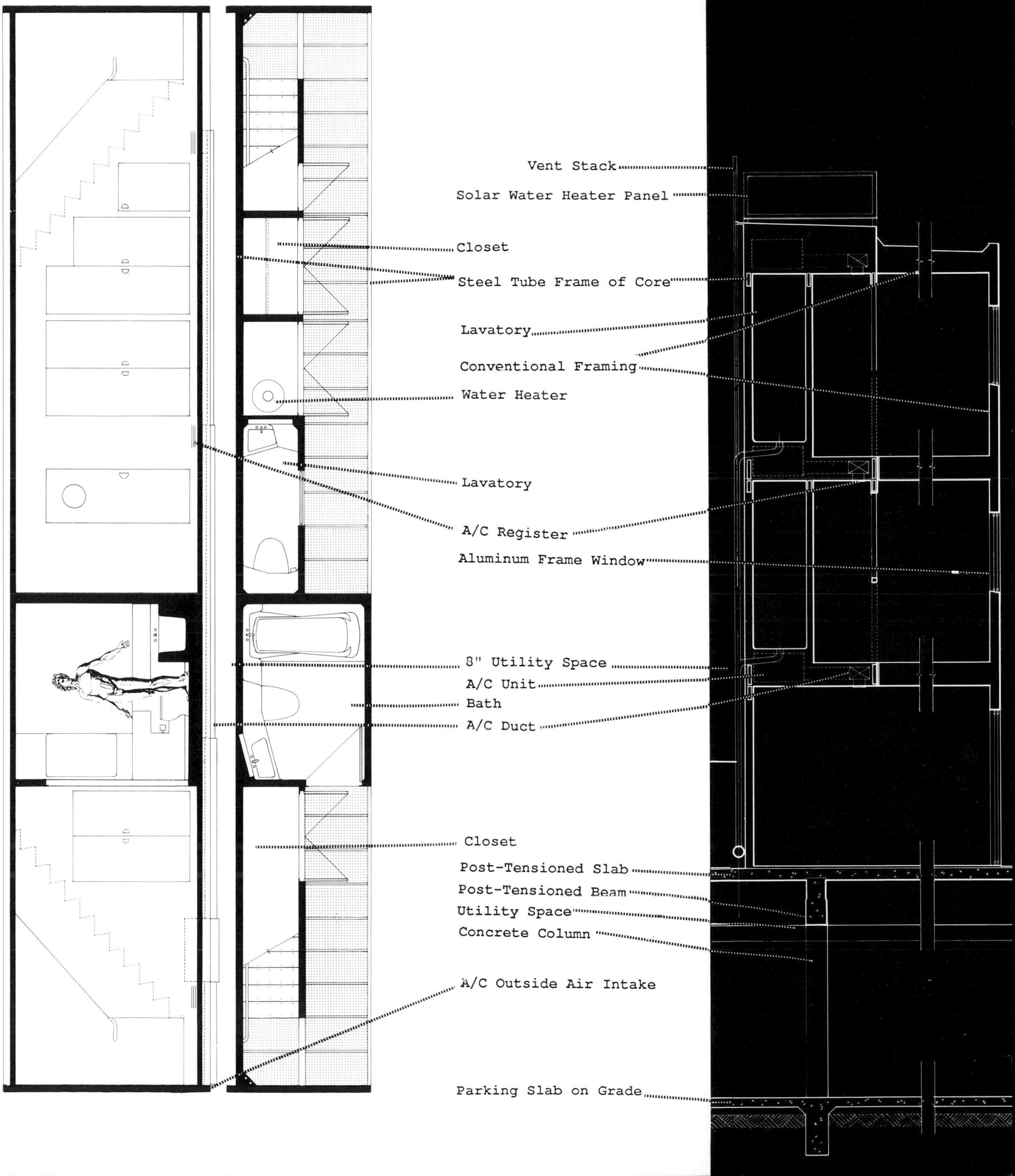

Vent Stack
Solar Water Heater Panel
Closet
Steel Tube Frame of Core
Lavatory
Conventional Framing
Water Heater
Lavatory
A/C Register
Aluminum Frame Window
8" Utility Space
A/C Unit
Bath
A/C Duct
Closet
Post-Tensioned Slab
Post-Tensioned Beam
Utility Space
Concrete Column
A/C Outside Air Intake
Parking Slab on Grade

Every architect is a social/urban planner by default. Obviously, every spatial configuration is steeped in attributes that impact its use and emotional ambience. Likewise, each pattern of access generates habitual patterns of use depending on scale and relation to the space. That we cannot accurately evaluate these effects in a straightforward way does not diminish their importance. On the contrary, their elusive nature compels us, as architects, to become more critical of the factors governing inhabitation rather than leaving them to chance or, worse, falling back on spatial constructs that no longer apply.

Assimilation of distinctive cultures has been a hallmark of contemporary society and a long-standing premise of modernism, whose proponents sought an abstract prototype for an ecumenical world. It now seems naive to speak of a uniform lifestyle in the face of a growing commitment to enhance and preserve cultural identity.

Migration, gender politics, the information society, and energy issues have created the need for a far more complex range of housing options than those advocated by modernists. Work at home, single parenthood, extended families, same-sex families, and the dramatically different spatial expectations of those from different cultural backgrounds have destroyed the "white bread" of commodity housing.

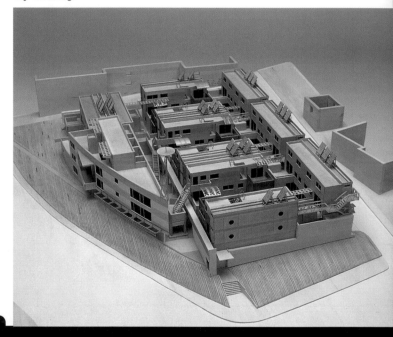

HEMDALE FILM CORPORATION AND OFFICE FACILITY, LOS ANGELES, 1990

An existing three-story building was renovated for the headquarters of an independent film company.

Common technical issues throughout this facility prompted the development of parallel systems for building components and furniture.

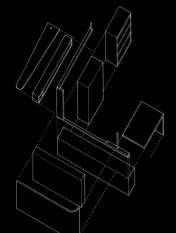

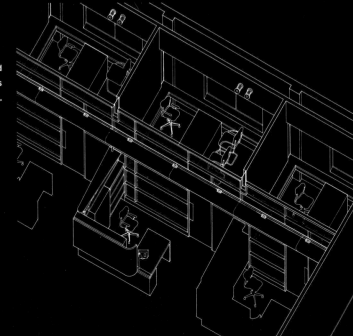

SOON THE CONSUMER WILL HAVE TO RESOLVE THE CONTEST BETWEEN THE CONTAINER
(PROVIDED BY THE ARCHITECT) AND THE CONTAINED (PROVIDED BY THE INDUSTRIAL DESIGNER).
IN THE PROJECT FOR FRANKLIN/LA BREA, THE CORE ELEMENTS ACT AS LARGE-SCALE
APPLIANCES TO ACTIVATE THE RELATIVELY NEUTRAL ARCHITECTURAL SPACE ADJACENT TO EACH.
THE RESULTING EQUATION EXPLOITS THE EFFICIENCIES IMPLICIT IN SERIAL PRODUCTION OF THE CORE
UNIT WHILE REINFORCING THE ROLE OF ARCHITECTURE.

A specially configured aluminum duct that defines the periphery of the open-office area channels energy, illumination, information, and conditioned air through a single component and deposits them at the desk of each worker. The desks and accessories share material and details with the duct.

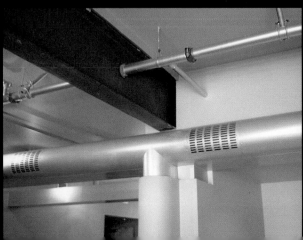

6:00

ALL COMPONENTS ARE FLEXIBLE, IF ONE IS WILLING TO SUSPEND THE OFTEN
DEFINING ROLE OF LANGUAGE AND SYMBOL.
       A CONVENIENT DEMONSTRATION IS THE PRACTICE
           OF SIMPLY RENAMING AN OTHERWISE UNDISTINGUISHED PRODUCT.
THIS SO-CALLED REBADGING, INVENTED BY THE AUTOMOBILE INDUSTRY,
      IS USED TO ASSIGN PROVENANCE AS A CYNICAL MARKET STRATEGY.
     THE TEST, OF COURSE, IS WHETHER A FLEXIBLE COMPONENT PERFORMS,
OCCUPIES SPACE, AND, MOST IMPORTANTLY, SUITS ITS USER AS WELL
AS A PURPOSE-BUILT ONE.

14:00

8:00

10:00

12:00

16:00

18:00

20:00

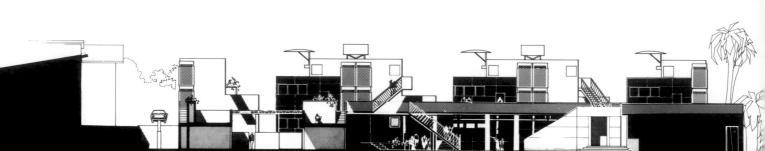

ONE COULD ARGUE THAT TECHNOLOGY IS THE MEANS TO AN END.
ONLY WHEN THAT END IS FIRMLY IN SIGHT
AND INEVITABLY PART OF THE TRANSACTIONS
OF ENERGY, CAPITAL, AND CULTURE
DO WE HAVE THE LUXURY TO CONSIDER ITS MERITS,
AND BY THEN IT IS TOO LATE.

**Longitudinal section
through "street"**

LINC HOUSING SYSTEM,
1969, U.S. PATENT NO. 3,605,354

A system of components was to be mass-produced for the construction of basic housing.

Our interest in automotive production technology led us to adapt the principles of spot welding to produce a mono-coque appliance/structure as the backbone of a prefabricated housing system. Such a component might incorporate mechanical and electrical devices common to housing as well as compartments for storage and circulation, cost-effective alternatives to the dead weight imposed by conventional engineering.

Racing cars employ a similar principle, reducing weight by assigning structural loads to mechanical compo-nents rather than letting them "go along for the ride."

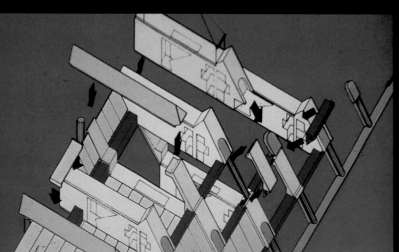

The original Case Study architects exemplified an approach to domestic architecture that echoed the generalized spatial concepts then coming into widespread use in the planning of high-rise office structures: a regular column grid, relatively long and consistent spans, and paneled cladding. Spatial divisions were transient and incidental to the larger construct. This was in sharp contrast to Irving Gill and Rudolph Schindler, whose balloon-frame structure was indivisible from the spatial construct and thus worked entirely within housing conventions.

Schindler and Gill's housing, particularly Schindler's Pueblo Ribera Court apartments (1923) in La Jolla, California, provided a working prototype for the apartments at Franklin/La Brea by demonstrating that public space, generally dominant in modernist as well as more traditional housing, could be replaced by a greatly expanded private domain. The courtyard and entry at the paseo are both intimate and sublime, giving the lie to the crowded effect conveyed by the bird's-eye view presented in published plans. The only loser is the largely symbolic "setting" for the building complex itself, which in Pueblo Ribera has been reduced to a single pedestrian-scale gate.

CREATIVE PLAYTHINGS RETAIL SHOP, NEW YORK, 1969

This flagship store for an innovative line of well-designed toys was located on East Fifty-third Street in Manhattan, adjacent to Paley Park.

Experiments with the scale of the manufacturer's line of children's toys led us to evolve a shelving system with self-contained lighting and a greater than normal face dimension. These blocks locked together to configure the space and to accommodate children, who were felt to be the shop's "real" customers.

Cost and weight were substantial hurdles to realizing the project until a visit to an exhibition of Donald Judd's sculpture led to a meeting with his fabricator—a sheet-metal shop whose main business was making air-conditioning ductwork.

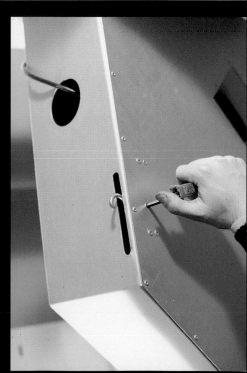

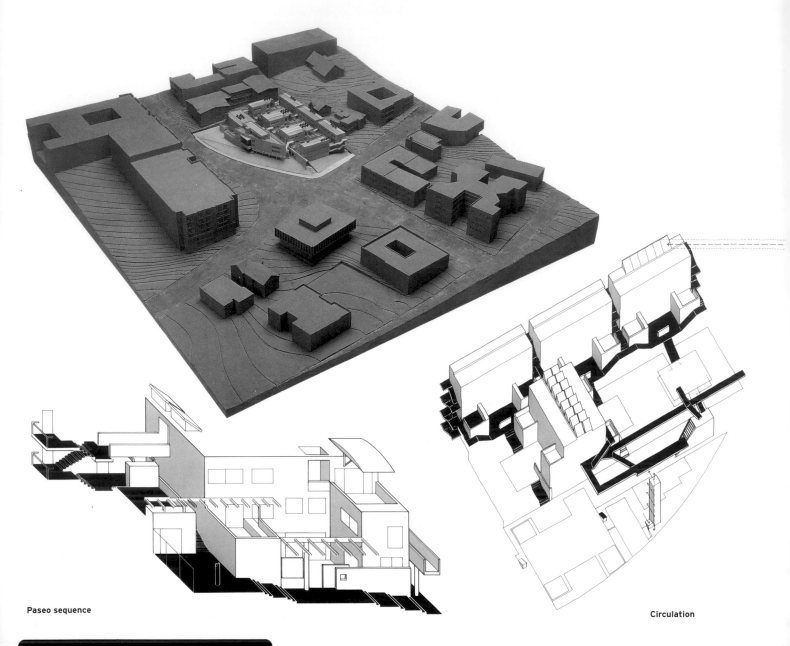

Paseo sequence

Circulation

AIRFRAME ALUMINUM FURNITURE,
GALLERY OF FUNCTIONAL ART, LOS ANGELES, 1991

We produced these prototypes in our workshop for an installation of architect-designed furniture. Each explored a particular fabrication technique that could be mass-produced.

A unique material composed of a plastic core sandwiched between thin metallic skins had lain around the office for some time before we defied a label that warned against heating and put it in the oven. Observing that it became very pliable before cooling to a rigid state, we immediately began imagining its potential for experiments in lightweight furniture, which we dubbed "Airframe." Comfort, ease of assembly, and an elegant translation of aircraft principles were our guides.

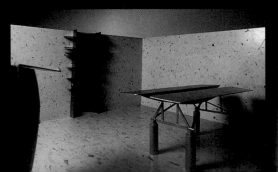

Framework

↑
N

REGRETTABLY, MOST ARCHITECTS HAVE BEGUN
TO SEE THE FUTURE THROUGH ONE ANOTHER'S EYES
RATHER THAN PURSUE.A VISION
SUITABLE TO SOCIETY'S CHANGING MORES, VALUES,
AND TECHNOLOGIES.
WHILE CIVILIZATIONS HAVE ALWAYS ADAPTED
THE OLD TO THE NEW, OFTEN WITH GREAT DIVIDENDS,
PROFOUND CHANGE OFFERS NO RECOURSE
BUT THE INVENTION OF AN ALTOGETHER NEW STRUCTURE.
ONE THINKS OF THE ELEVATOR,
WHICH WAS USED FOR YEARS TO CARRY HORSES
TO THE TOPS OF BUILDINGS, TO COHABIT THE ROOFS
WITH SERVANTS, UNTIL LE CORBUSIER SUGGESTED
THAT THE EQUATION OF SPACE
ITSELF HAD CHANGED.

Site plan

These experiments focused on the material's unique qualities in order to evolve a
particular set of fabrication techniques suited to production. Each technique generated
an exemplary item of furniture named after a historic aircraft.

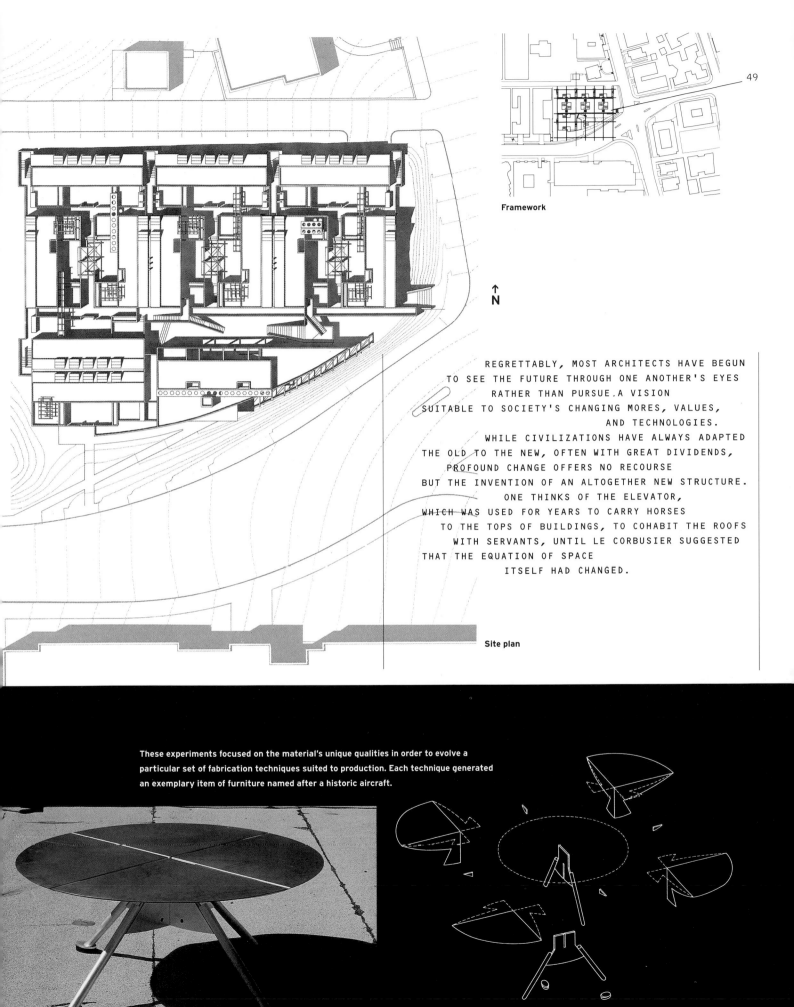

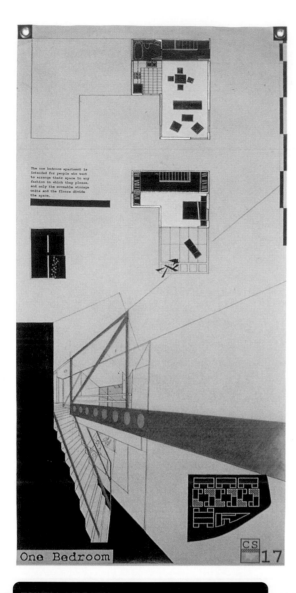

One Bedroom

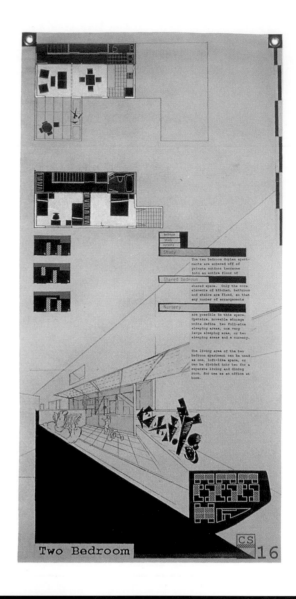

Two Bedroom

TOWELL LIBRARY,
UNIVERSITY OF CALIFORNIA AT LOS ANGELES, 1992

An immediate need for a temporary structure to house the university's undergraduate library required extensive prefabrication of components for this tensile structure.

From Japanese lanterns to birch-bark canoes to umbrellas: the principle of a tissue-thin covering over a rigid skeleton has been known and exploited for centuries, by nearly every culture. Rasterlike flexibility, enabling the description of complex forms by the simple expedient of regular sections, enabled us to explore a formal vocabulary limited only by what was appropriate and useful.

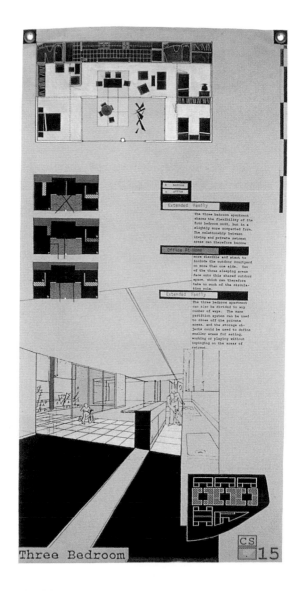

Three Bedroom

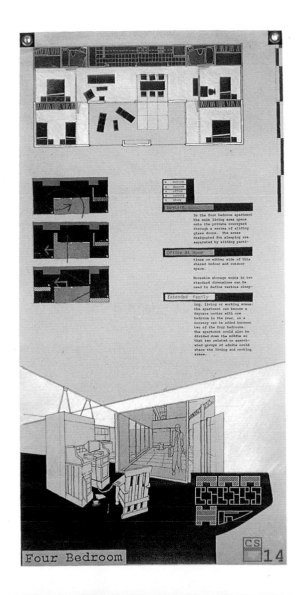

Four Bedroom

Bundles of ribs, designed in collaboration with the manufacturer, were custom-extruded to satisfy structural as well as architectural imperatives. Now bent to take their place in the building's form, they await completion of the foundations before being bolted into place.

The tapestry design for Franklin/La Brea evolved from the study of the field as a non-hierarchic spatial organization. Functional attributes are dispersed evenly throughout the domain rather than focused on a preferred location. We conceived of private outdoor space, equipment for food preparation and hygiene, workspace, shelter, and access as a continuous fabric. We extended Louis Kahn's premise of served and servant spaces to a broader spectrum of human activities in a genuinely democratic pattern.

We sought a balance between service elements defined by a production ethic/aesthetic (refrigerators, bath fixtures, etc.) and those that might involve the efforts of the user (storage, room assignment, enclosure, etc.). We attempted to parse out the utilitarian aspects of a typical apartment, amalgamate them beneath an industrialized rubric, then suggest that the volumetric domain of each dwelling is flexible and, most importantly, individual.

Thus we refined a production-based aesthetic, the search for meaningful spatial templates, and finally, an architectural discipline employing those differences to articulate a sense of place and human scale.

We looked toward an era when architecture could unite rather than divide those with different housing needs by encouraging the reidentification of living space according to individual need. Living rooms, bedrooms, and workrooms are shorn of fixed spatial consequences and surrendered to the occupants' whims.

We believe that a housing complex should validate each and every lifestyle, in the hope of creating at least a localized harmony.

PUNCH-OUT CARDBOARD FURNITURE, 1974

A line of furniture conceived for the mobile lifestyle then evolving among young people, the Punch-Out range was designed to leave room in the budget for records, food, and fun.

A fascination with the graphic space between the cutout parts of paper toys became a metaphor for the design of a range of cardboard furniture. Experimentation led to a set of designs that optimize material within a given sheet size. This in turn led us to envision marketing rows of slim packages, like books or records, which could be carried home and "punched-out" by the users, who we presumed would be young, mobile, and intelligent enough to realize that they shouldn't burden their lives with too many worldly goods (it was, after all, 1975).

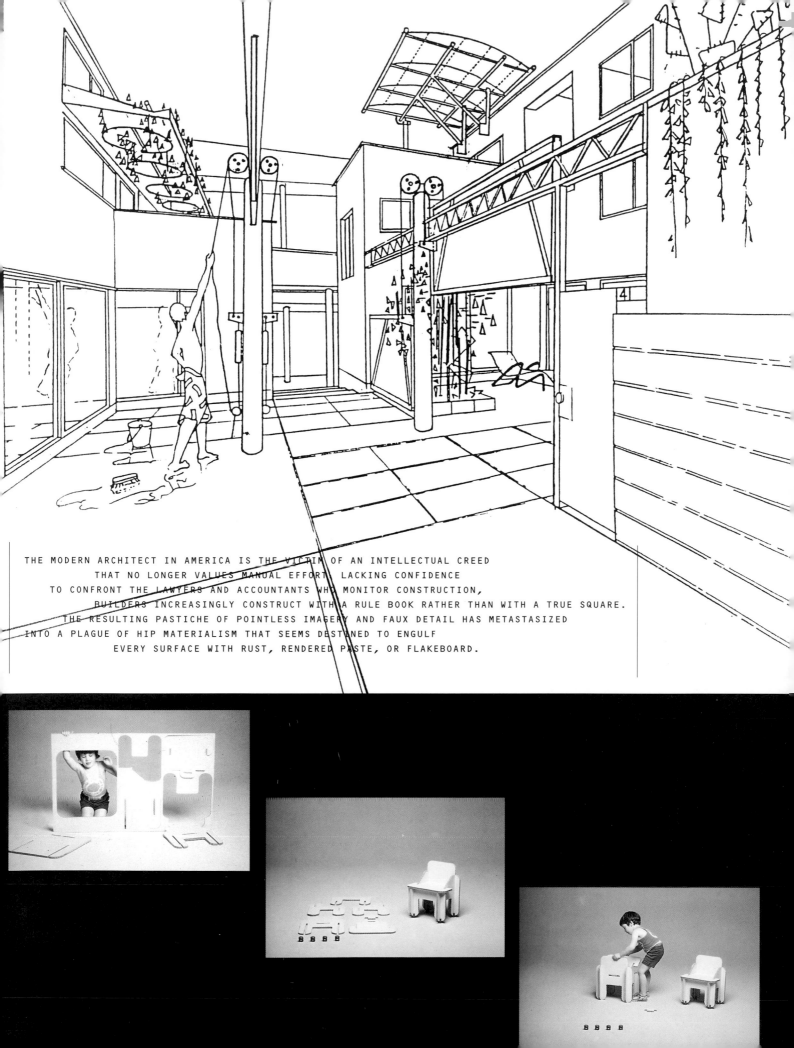

THE MODERN ARCHITECT IN AMERICA IS THE VICTIM OF AN INTELLECTUAL CREED
THAT NO LONGER VALUES MANUAL EFFORT. LACKING CONFIDENCE
TO CONFRONT THE LAWYERS AND ACCOUNTANTS WHO MONITOR CONSTRUCTION,
BUILDERS INCREASINGLY CONSTRUCT WITH A RULE BOOK RATHER THAN WITH A TRUE SQUARE.
THE RESULTING PASTICHE OF POINTLESS IMAGERY AND FAUX DETAIL HAS METASTASIZED
INTO A PLAGUE OF HIP MATERIALISM THAT SEEMS DESTINED TO ENGULF
EVERY SURFACE WITH RUST, RENDERED PASTE, OR FLAKEBOARD.

Rough Tech :

The Five Shrines were created for the opening exhibition

Decoding the Ordinary

of the World Financial Center in Lower Manhattan.
The exhibition brief stressed the relationship of the city to the
natural environment, prompting us to respond with **a set of
constructions that juxtapose the physical elements
of urban civilization with the natural
elements they often displace.**

Each element—temperature, decay, vegetation, earth, and sea—
was represented by a metaphoric construction supported by
a concrete-block pylon reminiscent of an office tower. We incorporated only
readily identifiable parts in order to communicate the pervasive
nature of the displacements.

We portrayed living matter via a colony of ants embedded in the soil,
a clump of wild grass, and a recording of the sounds of deep-sea mammals.
**Mechanical provisions in each case nurtured the living
components for the duration of the installation.**

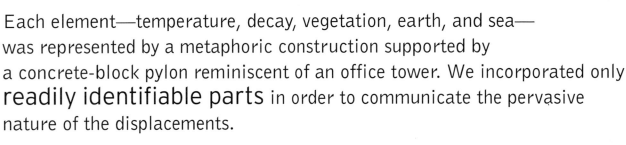

```
VALUE DEFINES APPLICATION.
        THE PROLIFERATION OF NEW GOODS IN UNRELATED MARKETS
    GENERATES VARIANTS THAT DIFFER IN VALUE AND DETAIL
            YET SHARE INDUSTRIAL DNA.
        CROSSBREEDS SUGGEST NOT ONLY RESILIENCE,
    BUT THE PRESENCE OF THE "OTHER," GENERIC STAND-INS
    FOR THE SAME OLD THING. A PLASTIC MILK CRATE EQUALS
            A CARDBOARD MILK CARTON - OR DOES IT?
```

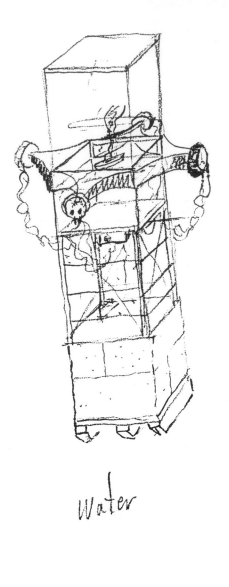

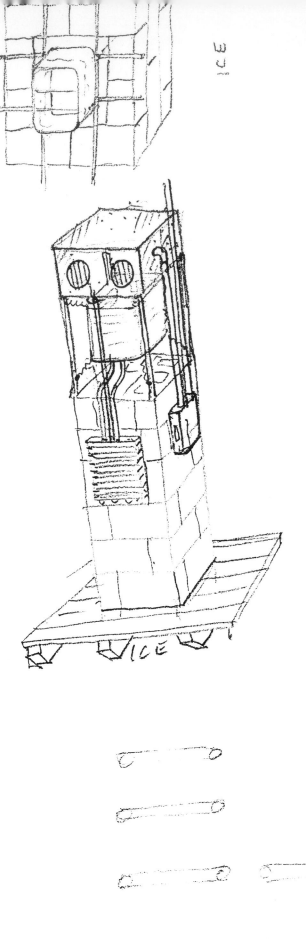

ICE

Water

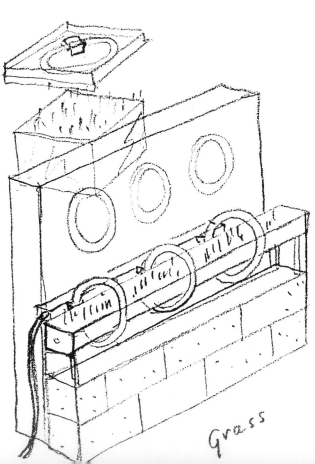

ICE

Grass

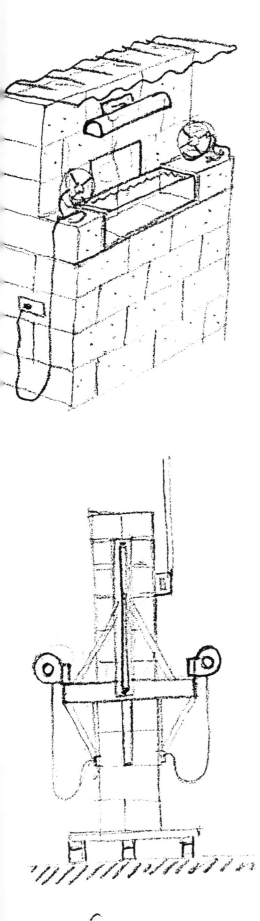

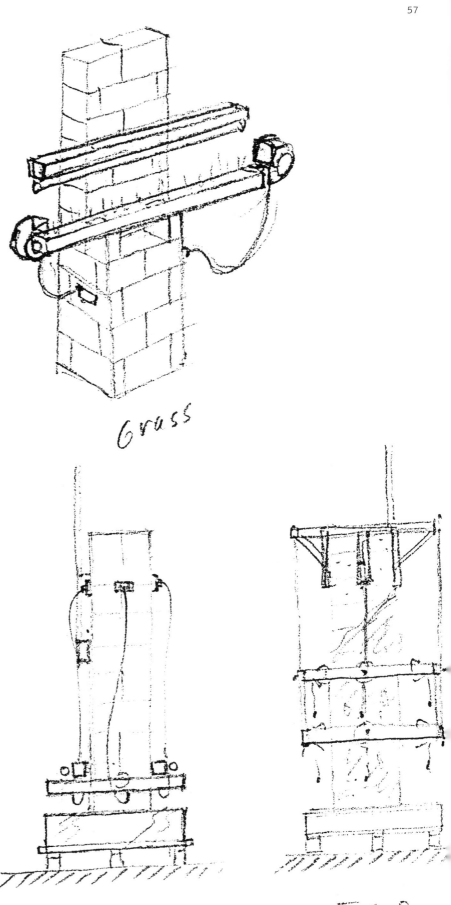

Grass

Grass

water

TAR

DIRT
A BLACK-AND-WHITE SURVEILLANCE CAMERA
SURPLUS LENSES
ROCK-FINISH LINOLEUM
FOUR PLASTIC ANT FARMS
A TEN-INCH BLACK-AND-WHITE TELEVISION
ALUMINUM STRUTS

THE SEA
A CHILDREN'S PLASTIC WADING POOL
AN AUTOMOBILE RADIO
AN ELECTRIC BULLHORN
BRINE
A SAWHORSE KIT
WIRE GLASS

GRASS
TWO FLOURESCENT GRO-LAMPS
CUSTOM ALUMINUM DUCT
GARDEN PEBBLE LINOLEUM
196 CUBIC INCHES OF TOPSOIL
KENTUCKY BLUEGRASS
DUAL YELLOW HAIR DRYERS

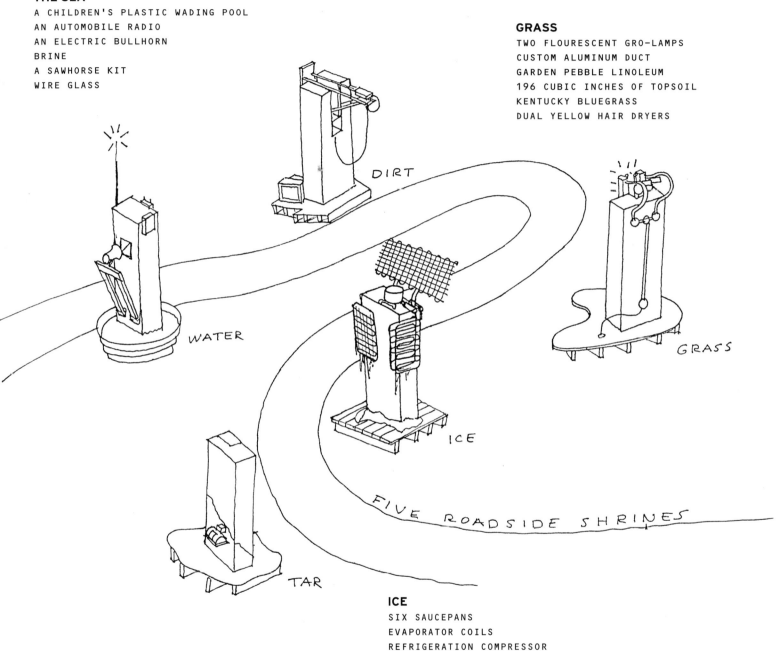

ICE
SIX SAUCEPANS
EVAPORATOR COILS
REFRIGERATION COMPRESSOR
GRID LINOLEUM

TAR
SLATE LINOLEUM
PROXIMITY SWITCH
TWO-HEAD BUG LAMP
TAR

The Five Shrines explored the realm of living things and their often quixotic relationship to the products of society. The life cycle, entropy, habitat, growth, and reproduction envelop and sustain the environment in which cities exist yet are eliminated in the quest for urbanity. These objects stand as metaphors for the drama of concrete versus wild grass, heavy equipment versus the anthill, runoff versus the open seas.

Industrial products further this incongruity: designed for our convenience, not that of the planet; suited to our habitat, not that of the beings displaced, they conform to a structural ethic rather than one of organic profusion.

In the Five Shrines we explored the consequences of an orderly integration of these products as an end in itself. We appraised each item, a common product in everyday use, for syntactic and formal meaning before allowing it to express the theme of the installation.

SOUTHSIDE SETTLEMENT COMMUNITY CENTER, COLUMBUS, OHIO, 1980

The Southside Settlement ethic emphasizes the use of common materials in common ways; hence only a few items are recognizably reencoded for unexpected functions.

Concrete finishing trowels serve as door pulls throughout the project.

THE EYE OF THE ARCHITECT
MUST ARRANGE STONES, SHELLS, AND GEMS
WITHOUT REGARD FOR VALUE.

61

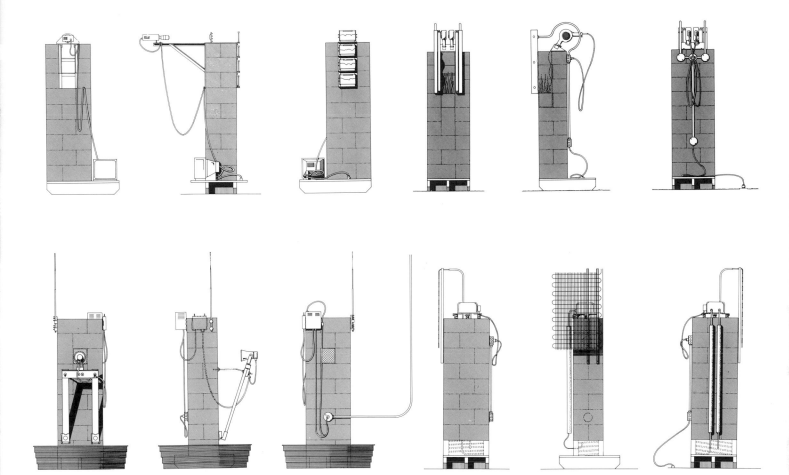

TOWELL LIBRARY, UNIVERSITY OF CALIFORNIA AT LOS ANGELES, 1992

The temporary nature of this construction permitted experimentation with unusual materials. The "shingled" planes of Lexan used for exterior glazing are clipped together with molded plastic buttons normally used for automobile upholstery.

The cylindrical element mimicking the rotonda of the building that Towell replaced is a prefabricated unit responsible for cooling the entire building.

Stair risers and air returns are made of a product used for industrial catwalks.

IN MUCH OF OUR WORK WE FIND THE ARCHITECTURAL IMPLICATIONS
OF THE PRAGMATIC ELEMENTS THAT PROVIDE SERVICES, ACCOMODATION,
AND STRUCTURE ENORMOUSLY SATISFYING.
THE STALLS, PACKAGE HVAC'S, BEARING PLATES, AND CHILLERS PROVIDE
MORE THAN ADEQUATE OPPORTUNITY TO ARTICULATE THE HUMANIST AGENDA
AT THE CORE OF ANY GREAT BUILDING.

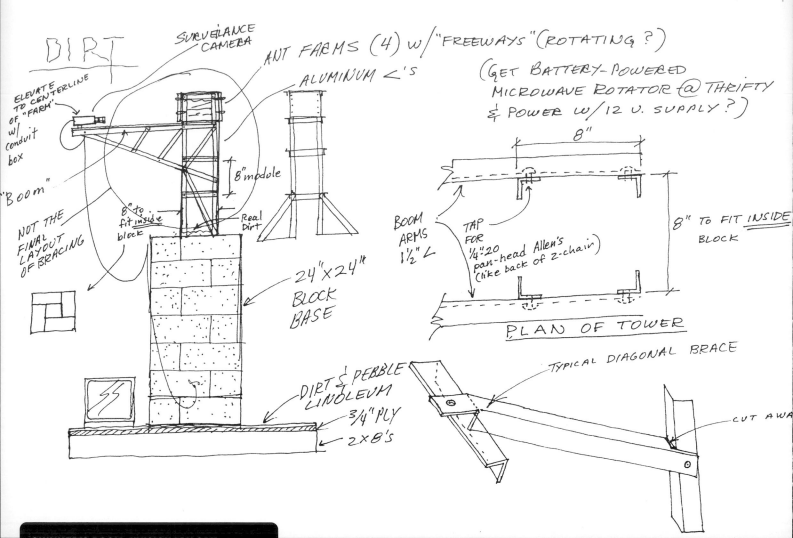

SKINNER'S ROOM, "VISIONARY SAN FRANCISCO," INSTALLATION, SAN FRANCISCO MUSEUM OF MODERN ART, 1991

The installation for Skinner's Room was devised for an exhibition at the San Francisco Museum of Modern Art in which writers and architects were asked to collaborate on visions of the city. William Gibson wrote a text in which the Bay Bridge becomes a metaphor for the social and ecological breakdown of the city. Such a city, he reasoned, would have been buffeted by speculation, entrepreneurs, and construction scavengers; racked by ethnic turf wars; and finally raped by foreign interests.

Our speculation focused on the specifics of a dystopian city; we created a city plan that incorporates physical evidence of its decline. Privatization of the public realm, evacuation of the urban core, and domination of the skyline by foreign interests provided a template for a city transformed.

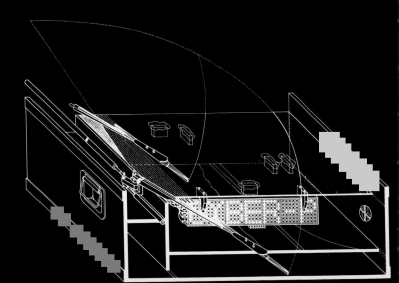

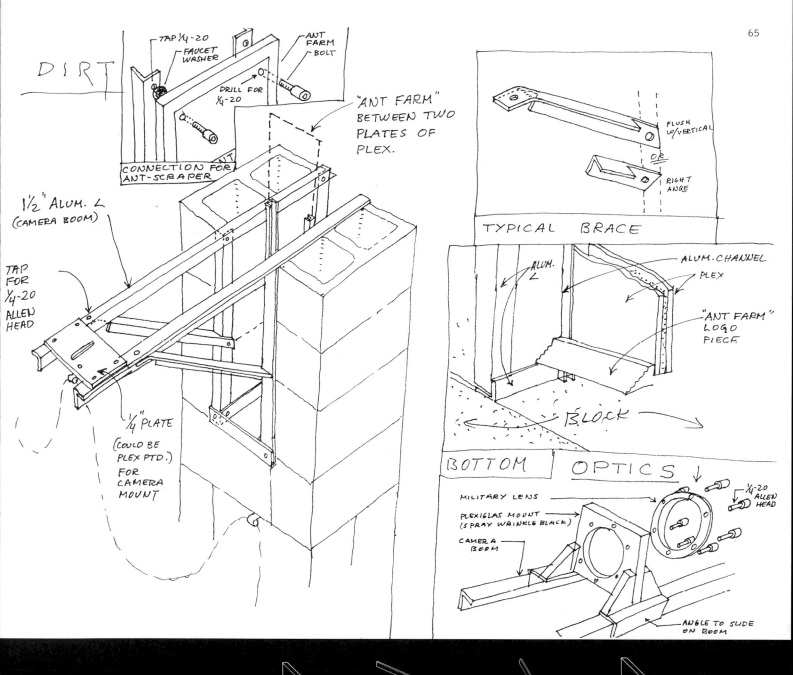

DIRT

TAP ¼-20
FAUCET WASHER
DRILL FOR ¼-20
ANT FARM BOLT

"ANT FARM" BETWEEN TWO PLATES OF PLEX.

CONNECTION FOR ANT-SCRAPER

1½" ALUM. L (CAMERA BOOM)

TAP FOR ¼-20 ALLEN HEAD

¼" PLATE (COULD BE PLEX PTD.) FOR CAMERA MOUNT

FLUSH W/VERTICAL
OR
RIGHT ANGE

TYPICAL BRACE

ALUM. L
ALUM. CHANNEL
PLEX
"ANT FARM" LOGO PIECE

BLOCK

BOTTOM | OPTICS

MILITARY LENS
PLEXIGLAS MOUNT (SPRAY WRINKLE BLACK)
CAMERA BOOM

¼-20 ALLEN HEAD

ANGLE TO SLIDE ON BOOM

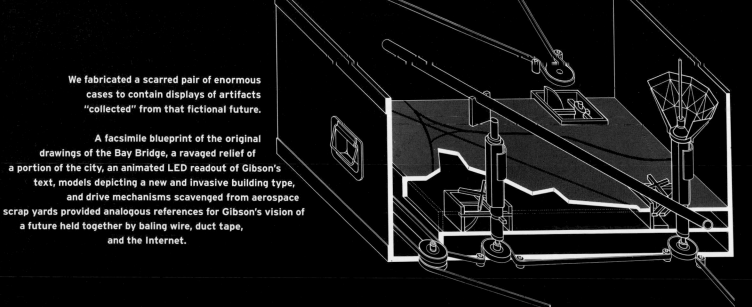

We fabricated a scarred pair of enormous cases to contain displays of artifacts "collected" from that fictional future.

A facsimile blueprint of the original drawings of the Bay Bridge, a ravaged relief of a portion of the city, an animated LED readout of Gibson's text, models depicting a new and invasive building type, and drive mechanisms scavenged from aerospace scrap yards provided analogous references for Gibson's vision of a future held together by baling wire, duct tape, and the Internet.

The shock of common objects in uncommon settings is a constant phenomenon in Gibson's stories. Here we were challenged to emulate the entropic decline of goods and mechanisms in a manner appropriate to the elusive meaning of Gibson's narrative, but also mechanically and visually illustrative of its emotional scope: a dystopian setting in which to affirm life and enduring human relationships.

Automobile windshield wipers whose rhythmic movement recalled the lyrics to "Me and Bobby McGee" set a key image for the installation, establishing the pervasive fog and the monotony of the Bay Bridge as metaphors for the displaced and dysfunctional denizens occupying its towers. The mechanism itself is united only in the fulfillment of its task—the futile reflexive sweep of a mechanical arm across a Plexiglas slate in a perfectly dry,

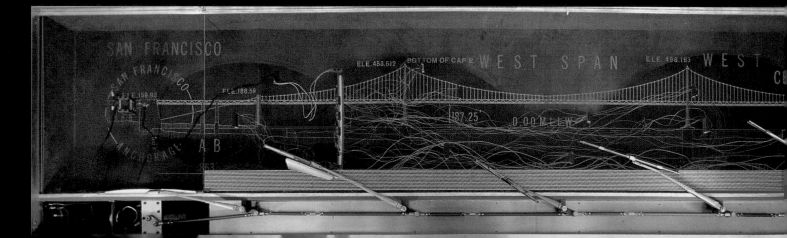

IN THE CONFINES OF THE FACTORY, THE ENGINEER VIEWS HIS STRUCTURE COLDLY.
HE SEES NO REASON TO TRANSFORM THE STRUTS AND FASTENERS
THAT MUST BE THERE OF NECESSITY, NOR DOES HE WISH TO CONCEAL THE TUBES AND SPRINGS
THAT OPERATE THE EQUIPMENT. HE IS SECURE IN HIS CRAFT, AND THE WORK
HE CONCEIVES HAS BOTH HONOR AND TRUTH. YET ASK HIM TO DESIGN A DWELLING
OR A PLACE OF BUSINESS, AND THIS ADMIRABLE CANDOR DISAPPEARS IN A PASTICHE
OF MOLDINGS AND PATTERNS THAT CONTRIBUTE LITTLE BUT COST TO THE ENTERPRISE.

air-conditioned environment. Below, in the dimly lit belly of the crate, a tangle of
circuitry—the disembowled guts of an electronic mother board and a gaggle of LED
readouts—endlessly reenacts the occupation of the bridge.

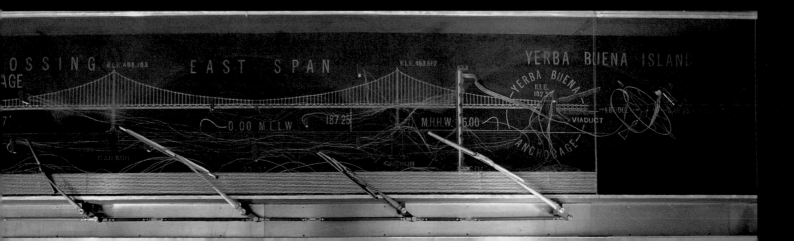

The general-purpose fittings in the typical hardware store offer significant constraints for serious design. Aside from a few highly optimized fasteners and the accidental charm of the "kit of parts," the conventions established by a hardware-store sensibility make truly efficient construction both unlikely and impossibly adversarial. While such items are products of a relatively sophisticated manufacturing process, their applications are so generic that a refined relationship to end product is highly improbable.

Yet the art of assemblage or of the exploitation of the subtext implicit in even off-the-shelf hardware, applied to an architectural object, suggests that even mundane objects can contribute to an aesthetic "message."

All modern buildings are assemblies of manufactured articles and a number of more or less tailor-made transitions. One can accept that and accommodate the "designed" reality to the practical reality on a case-by-case basis, or one can reject it, segregating reality and abstract logic in the pursuit of an aesthetic or practical ideal. The Five Shrines proposed forthright divisions between static construction composed of mass and volume, dynamic accessories dependent on time or position, and natural exhibits.

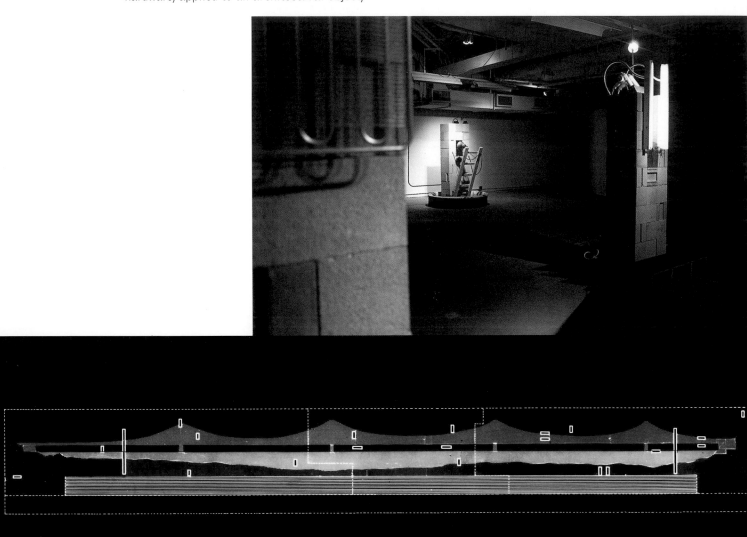

THE AUDIENCE FOR SYMBOLIC CONTENT
WAS SIMILARLY ATTRACTED TO THE
CADILLAC AUTOMOBILE LONG AFTER IT
HAD LOST ALL OF ITS ORIGINAL CHARACTER
BUT THE NAME AND THE CREST.
WHAT OPPORTUNITIES HAVE BEEN MISSED
IN THE PRACTICE OF TRADING
IN SYMBOLIC CONTENT WHEN WELL-KNOWN
ALTERNATIVES THAT PERFORM BETTER
AND MORE CONVENIENTLY EXIST?

This project offered a rare opportunity to explore the other side of an architectural utopia.
Failed ideas, worn-out materials, and dysfunctional places don't often find their way into
an architectural genre.

Here the carcass of a worn-out San Francisco is reclaimed by predators. A luxury community surrounds and privatizes Golden Gate Park, an entertainment company claims and "themes" the Presidio, a condo-consortia plants optimized solar-powered towers in an inexorable march across the Tenderloin, and a container-dock shopping district is carved out of the Candlestick.

ALL MANUFACTURED PRODUCTS HAVE UNSTATED, THOUGH EQUALLY CONVINCING
ALTERNATIVE USES THAT THE DESIGNER MAY UNCOVER AND APPLY.
WILLIAM GIBSON SUGGESTS THAT AN AUTO STARTER MOTOR
         PROVIDE POWER FOR AN ELEVATOR.
            A BIRD'S FEATHER BECOMES A QUILL PEN;
            A CAR TIRE PROTECTS BOATS FROM THE PIER.
         ROBERT PIRSIG, IN ZEN AND THE ART OF MOTORCYCLE MAINTENANCE,
            TELLS OF A REJECTED SHIM MADE OF A SYNTACTICALLY
                  INCORRECT ALUMINUM BEER CAN.
      ARCHITECTS CAN EXPLOIT SUCH OPPORTUNITIES,
      WHICH ARE DRIVEN OUT OF THE MASS MARKET BY ECONOMIES OF SCALE.

Our concept for this exhibition **Experience** illuminated the evolution of the Case Study houses of the 1950s and the postwar lifestyle that they were designed to nurture.

Charles and Ray Eames, Craig Ellwood, Eero Saarinen, and others exemplified an American-style ingenuity unfettered by tradition and eager to translate the fruits of wartime technology into peacetime utility. Design and architecture then were deeply affected by changing roles and shifting priorities. We sought to contrast the designer's centrality then with the marginal role that design occupies today.

The exhibition, at The Museum of Contemporary Art's Temporary Contemporary facility in downtown Los Angeles, occupied 36,000 square feet. We were determined to present architecture's typically high-brow aspirations in a way that would entertain and educate, rather than mystify. Thus the exhibition design emphasized the visitors' experience, enveloping them in period ambience while revealing the architects' social and technical agenda.

and Scenario

BLUEPRINTS FOR MODERN LIVING

History and Legacy of the Case Study Houses

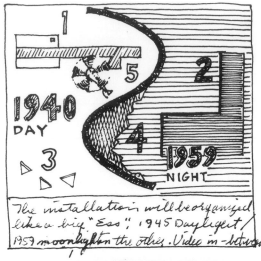

The installation will be organized like a big "Ess", 1945 Daylight/ 1959 moonlight on the other. Video in-between.

in a thick wall which is also a cyclorama and a display and circulation means and information.

Entering, Ralph Rapson's 1945 proto-type glows in the sun. Mom is hanging up the laundry. Dad is in the Helicopter.

In the moonlight... video biographies of all 21 houses will hang like the lights of the city...

So that, looking down from the Koenig house living room the horizon will sparkle w/ life!

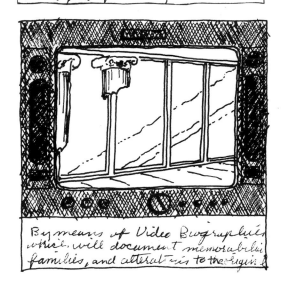

By means of Video Biographies which will document memorabilia families, and alterations to the origin

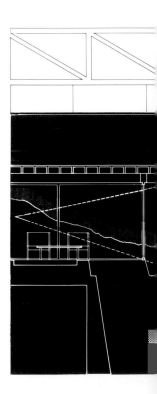

CASE STUDY HOUSE
No. 22

A continuous cyclorama dividing the space into realms representing
day and night signaled the beginning and the end
of the Case Study era.

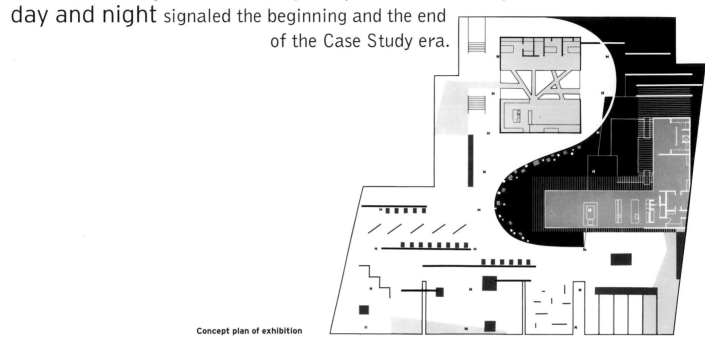

Concept plan of exhibition

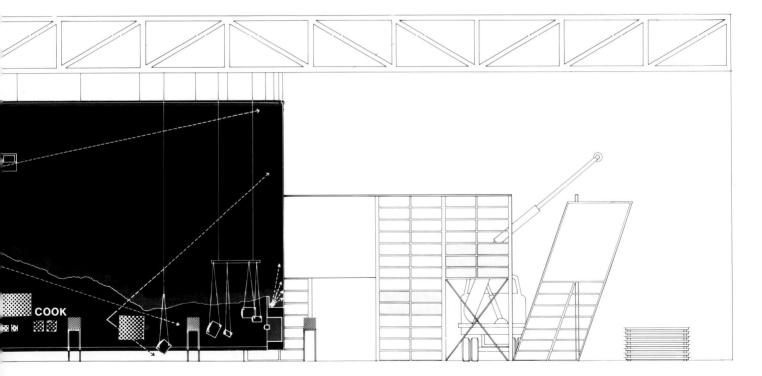

COOK

FE STYLE DISPLAY   **MONITOR INTERVIEWS**   **CASE STUDY MODELS**   **EAMES HOUSE PROCESS**

VIDEOTAPED INTERVIEWS WITH INDIV-
IDUALS ASSOCIATED WITH THE CASE
STUDY HOUSE PROGRAM WILL BE INTER-
SPERSED WITH VIDEO MATERIAL DOC-
UMENTING ASPIRATIONS AND CIRCUM-
STANCES OF THE PERIOD.

DETAILED MODELS OF THE 24 COMPLETED
HOUSES AND 12 PROJECTS WILL BE
ARRANGED IN A CHRONOLOGICAL GRID
TO ILLUMINATE THE SINGULAR NATURE
OF THE PROGRAM AS A WHOLE.

A STEP-BY-STEP DEMONSTRATION
OF THE ERECTION OF PREFABRICATED
COMPONENTS FROM WHICH THE HOUSE IS
CONSTRUCTED TO ITS FINAL ELABORATION
BY THE EAMES' OWN COLLECTION OF
DECORATIVE ARTIFACTS.

Above: Pierre Koenig,
Case Study House #22,
1959.
(Photo: Julius Shulman)

Left: Full-scale replica of
Case Study House #22
in "Blueprints for Modern
Living" exhibition.

Pierre Koenig, Case Study
House #22, 1959.
(Photo: Julius Shulman)

Two full-scale replicas of historically significant
houses, Case Study houses #4 by Ralph Rapson and # 22 by Pierre Koenig,
nestled on either side of the cyclorama, provided tangible evidence
of the inhabitants' lifestyle. Radios were "tuned" to period stations.
Toys, breakfast foods, and magazines vied for attention on the kitchen tables,
while furnishings and artifacts reflected the exuberant transformation
of such things as military nose cones into domestic lamps
and fiberglass reinforcement into luminous draperies.

Video documentation created especially for the exhibit captured the firsthand experiences of architects, clients, and builders alike as they struggled to define goals for their houses, or to hurdle over long-forgotten obstacles.

As designers, we found meaningful parallels in their experience, which encouraged us to emulate many of the premises embodied in the Case Study projects. Installation design motifs recalled specific building elements drawn from the program, recomposed to suggest their significance to a contemporary audience.

The "Blueprints" exhibition offered an opportunity to reassert principles of legibility and utility that had become obscure or at least unfashionable in the indulgent designs of the 1980s. As such, it voiced a mild rebuke to the prevailing critical climate, which equates the art in architecture with overt displays of angst-ridden fastenings, iconoclastic textures, and obsessive decor.

John Entenza, the Eameses, and the others clearly reasoned that purposeful design was not only compatible with what has come to exemplify the California lifestyle but was in fact its natural complement—like dune buggies, skateboards, and camping gear. We sought to emulate the idea of reason and economy in the support of content, stripping the installation components down to a single gesture that would set the stage for the show.

We convinced MOCA director Richard Koshalek that full-scale replications of exemplary Case Study houses were essential to engage the popular imagination, but he was understandably nervous about placing a building within the Temporary Contemporary and the architectural conflicts that might arise.

We were working at the time on a special effects film project and had become familiar with theatrical backings. Vast spaces can be simulated by cycloramas. This seemed the ideal device to "relocate" the replica in a redefined space within the Temporary Contemporary. The S-shape of the aluminum "curtain," black on one side and illuminated with a graphic timeline on the other, created a viable backdrop for each replica house, flaunting a technical kinship with Rapson's house and enveloping Koenig's in a satisfying darkness, illuminated only by period lighting and the glow of an array of monitors below.

We adopted scenographic principles routinely employed in theme parks, exploiting the narrative structure of the theme park while avoiding its eclectic styling. Carefully orchestrated spatial relationships plunged visitors into a totality in which the environment, artifacts, and ephemera of the period evoked a coherent reality.

INVITED COMPETITION, EXPANSION PLAN FOR THE UNIVERSAL AMPHITHEATER, UNIVERSAL CITY, CALIFORNIA, 1995

The grounds surrounding the existing Universal Amphitheater had become landlocked by competing attractions at Universal City, and required expansion. Our winning design for the new facility forms around the dramatic sequence of concert events: pre-show, performance, and after-the-show.

A video arcade points across a lagoon to an array of front and rear projection screens. Parallax creates unfolding sight lines leading to booths and kiosks. Images hover on water vapor.

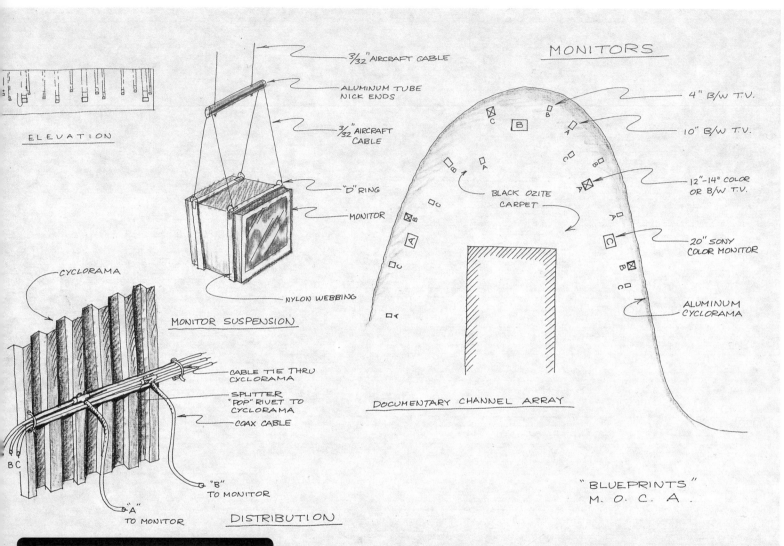

ELEVATION

3/32" AIRCRAFT CABLE

ALUMINUM TUBE NICK ENDS

3/32" AIRCRAFT CABLE

"D" RING

MONITOR

NYLON WEBBING

MONITOR SUSPENSION

CYCLORAMA

CABLE TIE THRU CYCLORAMA

SPLITTER "POP" RIVET TO CYCLORAMA

COAX CABLE

B C

"B" TO MONITOR

"A" TO MONITOR

DISTRIBUTION

MONITORS

4" B/W T.V.

10" B/W T.V.

12"-14" COLOR OR B/W T.V.

20" SONY COLOR MONITOR

BLACK OZITE CARPET

ALUMINUM CYCLORAMA

DOCUMENTARY CHANNEL ARRAY

"BLUEPRINTS" M.O.C.A.

INVITED COMPETITION, VESEY PLACE, BATTERY PARK CITY, NEW YORK, 1994

This public square in Lower Manhattan is to act as the keystone of the intensive residential, commercial, and office development surrounding the World Financial Center. Our scheme envisions a marketplace, playground, and park assembled as a collage of experiences that bring residents and office workers together.

Stalls act as neighborhood docks for a fleet of artist-designed trucks offering espresso, books, flowers, and snacks. The glass-and-steel canopy and the white tile floor recall the facades of the slaughterhouses that once occupied the area.

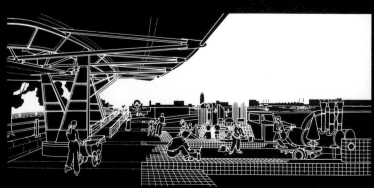

A traditional park, elevated just above traffic and surrounded by an emblematic railing, provides shade and a place to read. The diagonal axes of its paths reassert the hidden grid of Wall Street.

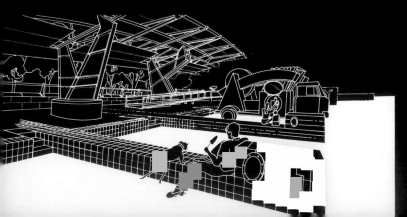

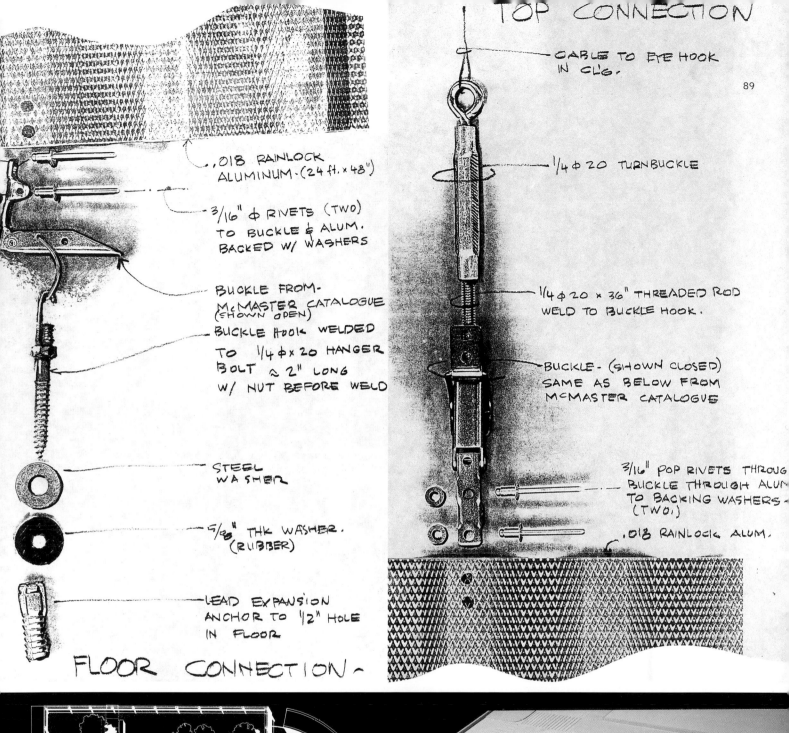

.018 RAINLOCK
ALUMINUM. (24 ft. × 48")

3/16" φ RIVETS (TWO)
TO BUCKLE & ALUM.
BACKED W/ WASHERS

BUCKLE FROM
MᶜMASTER CATALOGUE
(SHOWN OPEN)

BUCKLE HOOK WELDED
TO 1/4 φ × 20 HANGER
BOLT ≈ 2" LONG
W/ NUT BEFORE WELD

STEEL
WASHER

5/8" THK WASHER.
(RUBBER)

LEAD EXPANSION
ANCHOR TO 1/2" HOLE
IN FLOOR

FLOOR CONNECTION ~

CABLE TO EYE HOOK
IN CLG.

1/4 φ 20 TURNBUCKLE

1/4 φ 20 × 36" THREADED ROD
WELD TO BUCKLE HOOK.

BUCKLE - (SHOWN CLOSED)
SAME AS BELOW FROM
MᶜMASTER CATALOGUE

3/16" POP RIVETS THROUGH
BUCKLE THROUGH ALUM
TO BACKING WASHERS
(TWO)

.018 RAINLOCK ALUM.

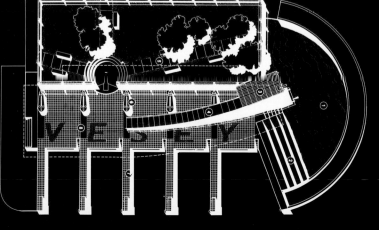

Viewed from the surrounding towers, an
etched-glass pattern casts the name Vesey

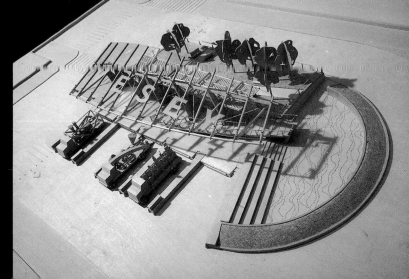

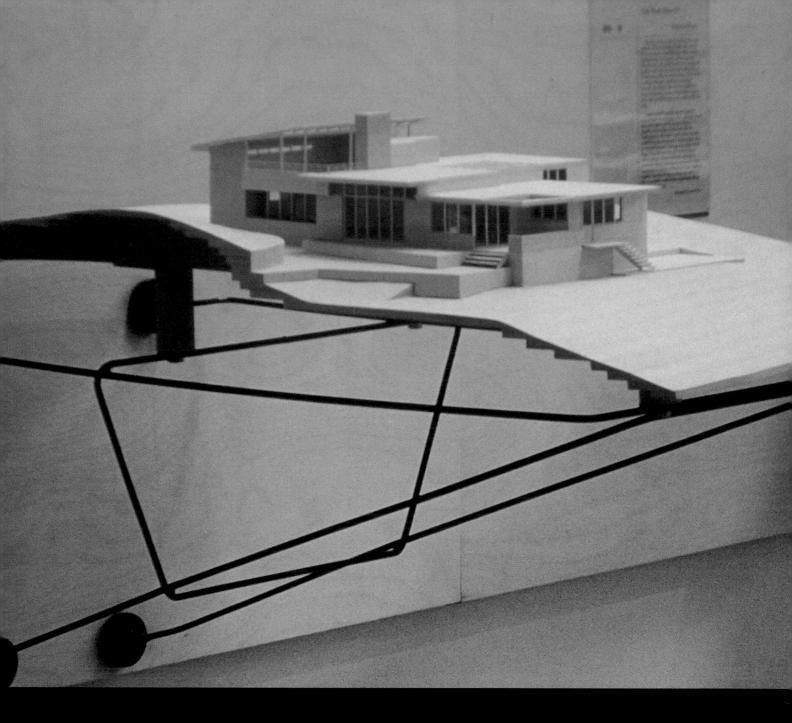

ROCKPLEX

ROCK IS IMMEDIATE.

ROCK IS NOW.

THE ENTRANCE TO ROCK WORLD COULD BE HERE JUST FOR TODAY.

AN OPEN SCAFFOLD VIBRATES WITH IMPATIENT CHANTING, BRILLIANT STABS OF LIGHT, AND SOUND CHECKS FROM AN ABOUT-TO-BEGIN STADIUM CONCERT.

AT ROCK WORLD, A BACKSTAGE PASS IS WORTH ITS WEIGHT IN GOLD, BUT YOU CAN OBTAIN ONE FROM THE "SCALPERS" WHO WORK A CUSTOM TOUR BUS AND SEMI-RIG COVERED WITH PSYCHEDELIC GRAPHICS.

UNDER THE SCAFFOLD, A HUGE VIDEO SCREEN HAS BEEN LOWERED TO THE GROUND FOR REPAIR. SAMPLE CLIPS BLAST INTERMITTENT IMAGES FROM PAST CONCERTS AS

HODGETTS + FUNG

BACKSTAGE MUST BE EXPERIENCED BY A TRIP ON ROCK WORLD'S CUSTOMIZED ELEVATORS. LONG BLACK STRETCH LIMOS LOWER YOU TO THE DEPTHS OF THE "LOOP".

'FOUND' SPACES IN DESERTED METAL FACTORY BUILDINGS RING WITH RAP AND THE STACATTO BEAT OF SYNTHESIZERS.

JUMP ON THE HEAVY METAL CONVEYOR FOR A TRIP THROUGH ROCK

MEMORIES, AND A TRIP TO THE TROPICANA.

IN ITS RECORDING STUDIOS YOU MAY ENCOUNTER A GHOST PERFORMANCE BY A FAVORITE BAND LIKE THE ROLLING STONES WHERE THE GHOSTLY IMAGES OF MICK AND HIS BLOKES APPEAR TO PLAY REAL INSTRUMENTS.

WOOD HOTEL WAS A MAJOR HANG-OUT FOR THE UP-AND-COMING, A PARTY SPOT FOR WANNABES, AND THE LAST STOP FOR HAS-BEENS.

H F

GUESTS MAY STAY IN ROOMS LIKE THESE, ENJOY DRINKS AND FOOD AROUND THE CLASSIC POOL, OR ASCEND TO THE ALIEN MOTHERSHIP WHICH HOVERS ABOVE TO ENJOY THE PAST AND FUTURE OF ROCK AND ROLL.

OR YOU MAY JOIN YOUR FAVORITE SINGER IN A HOLOGRAPHIC KARAOKE BAR. PUNCH THE RIGHT BUTTON AND YOU CAN HEAR THE VOICES OF LONG-GONE D.J.'S MIX ALL THE GREAT ONES JUST LIKE THEY USED TO.

FINALLY, REC... MEMORIES AND ... DOWN OUT OF ... CLOUDS IN A S... VAN.

ROCKPLEX ENTERTAINMENT CENTER,
UNIVERSAL CITY, CALIFORNIA, 1990

In this project for an entertainment center
we sought to fuse architecture, narrative
experience, and musical performance.
The metaphorical setting was to contain replicas
of the venues for significant musical events,
state-of-the-art media,
and a significant collection of artifacts.

A storyboard illustrated the major components
of Rockplex. The substitution of a temporary
scaffolding for a traditional, monumental
building facade reflects our conviction that
the world of music might best be represented

Films like <u>Blade Runner</u> and <u>Metropolis</u> explore such imaginary environments. Given few structural or financial constraints, such films can approximate the experience of what may be a purely theoretical architecture.

<u>Blade Runner</u> owes much to Archigram's visions, and the outer-space environments in <u>2001: A Space Odyssey</u> draw on Joe Colombo's experiments. Yet architecture, because of (or in spite of) its longevity, bridges the moments that film can only locate. Film dwells in the moment when light and action and point of view coincide to produce a perfect mesh of vision and emotion, while architecture exists in a continuum of solar motion, circumstance, and individual destiny. Accidental relationships prevail, whether of context or evolution. Still, the arsenal of scenographic devices affords a compelling discipline to break the deadlock of architectural style and the explosive pluralism of contemporary society.

AST COMPUTERS, EXHIBITION DESIGN, 1992

The introduction of new computers at the annual COMDEK tradeshow in Las Vegas requires ingenuity to attract potential buyers. We devised this scenario for the introduction of AST's highly sophisticated new unit.

A heavily modified bus with no windows makes the rounds of area hotels to pick up conventioneers and take them to a remote location.

Aboard the bus, a rear projection screen divides passengers from the driver, providing the illusion of a journey through an increasingly desolate landscape.

Disembarking in an underground cavern, the travelers confront a huge, primitive computer god (similar to the Trojan Horse). Worshippers appear to be imprisoned by an enormous stockade.

A luminous "electronic" realm filled with music is on the other side. One can journey there, but only by passing through an "information tunnel" that explains the advantages of AST's technology.

The mistress of ceremonies conducts activities from atop a giant, motorized chariot encircled by an electrical flux. She is the natural enemy of the computer god. When the worshippers drag the god through the stockade, she destroys it to protect her realm.

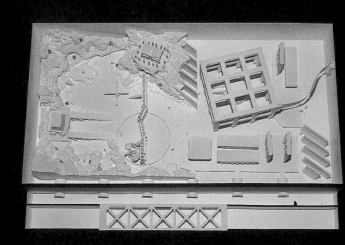

INVITED COMPETITION, LOS ANGELES ARTS PARK,
SEPULVEDA BASIN, LOS ANGELES, CALIFORNIA, 1989

DESIGN PARTNERS: ADÈLE NAUDÉ SANTOS,
CHARLES PEARSON AND MARK RIOS (LANDSCAPE),
MARY MISS (ARTIST)

A Place for

The Los Angeles Arts Park is to place the arts in a late-twentieth-century context and to bring **cultural focus** to a region historically recognized for **suburban sprawl**. Our design encourages a fruitful interaction among the converging disciplines of

Encounter

theater, visual art, music, and mass communication. The adjacent outdoor recreational facilities are integral to the overall experience.

To recall the history of the site and establish a coherent identity, our proposal anticipates the replanting of the orange groves once prevalent in the area. These groves, together with the associated irrigation equipment, form a visible sign of the park and a canopy of shade uniting the diverse facilities.

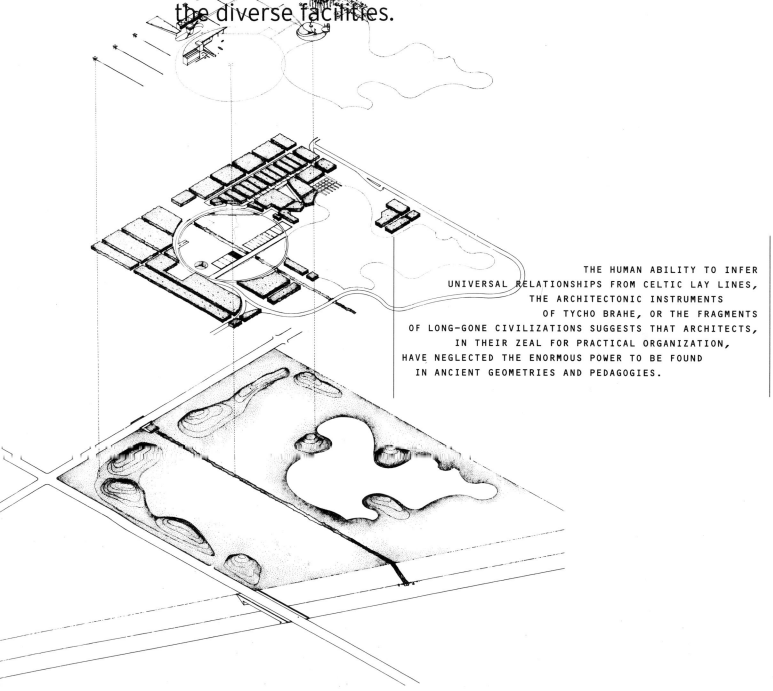

THE HUMAN ABILITY TO INFER UNIVERSAL RELATIONSHIPS FROM CELTIC LAY LINES, THE ARCHITECTONIC INSTRUMENTS OF TYCHO BRAHE, OR THE FRAGMENTS OF LONG-GONE CIVILIZATIONS SUGGESTS THAT ARCHITECTS, IN THEIR ZEAL FOR PRACTICAL ORGANIZATION, HAVE NEGLECTED THE ENORMOUS POWER TO BE FOUND IN ANCIENT GEOMETRIES AND PEDAGOGIES.

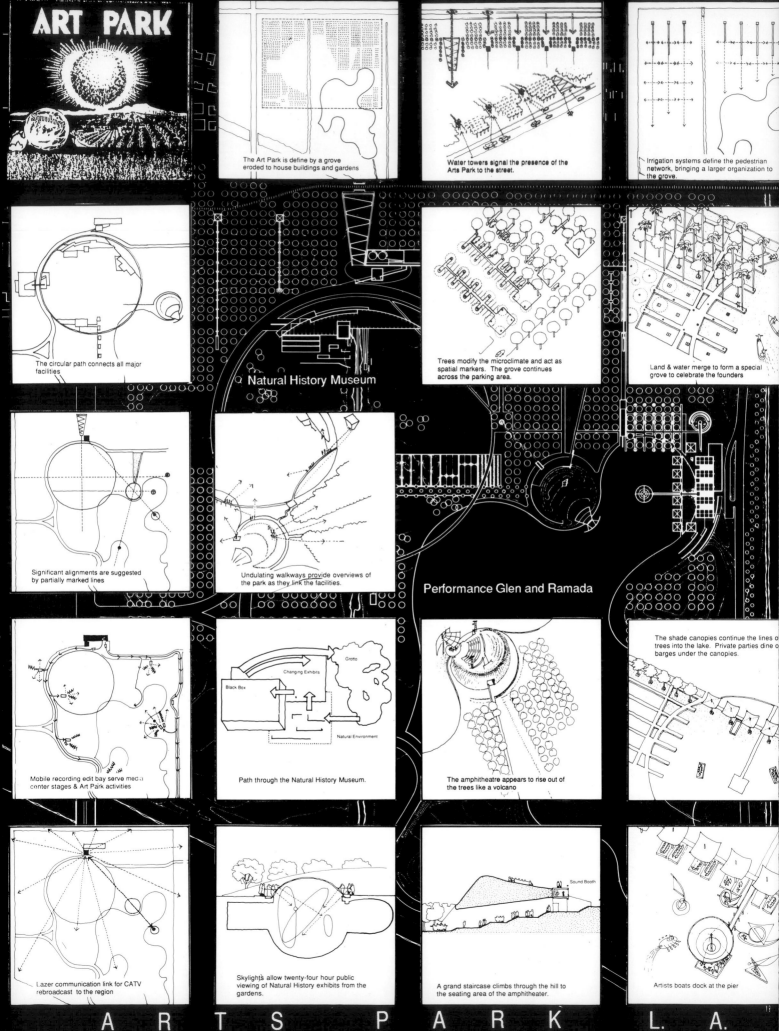

ART PARK

The Art Park is define by a grove eroded to house buildings and gardens

Water towers signal the presence of the Arts Park to the street.

Irrigation systems define the pedestrian network, bringing a larger organization to the grove.

The circular path connects all major facilities

Natural History Museum

Trees modify the microclimate and act as spatial markers. The grove continues across the parking area.

Land & water merge to form a special grove to celebrate the founders

Significant alignments are suggested by partially marked lines

Undulating walkways provide overviews of the park as they link the facilities.

Performance Glen and Ramada

Mobile recording edit bay serve media center stages & Art Park activities

Changing Exhibits

Grotto

Black Box

Natural Environment

Path through the Natural History Museum.

The amphitheatre appears to rise out of the trees like a volcano

The shade canopies continue the lines of trees into the lake. Private parties dine on barges under the canopies.

Lazer communication link for CATV rebroadcast to the region

Skylights allow twenty-four hour public viewing of Natural History exhibits from the gardens.

Sound Booth

A grand staircase climbs through the hill to the seating area of the amphitheater.

Artists boats dock at the pier

A R T S P A R K L. A.

THE PHYSICAL ELEMENTS POPULATING SUCH LANDSCAPES BECOME ACTIVE PARTS
OF A DRAMA. EMOTIONAL, HISTORIC, AND SYMBOLIC CONTENT IS
WOVEN INTO THEIR ARRANGEMENT, THEIR TEXTURE, THEIR CONFIGURATION.
THE VISITOR'S IMAGINATION ENGAGES THAT OF THE ARCHITECT.

The site is organized around a **circular promenade,** which creates a clear relationship among the buildings (to be designed by various architects and thus not immediately predictable) and provides an icon for the park as a whole. A man-made lake flows beneath the promenade to the south, forming a contained inlet and punctuated by a short, curving bridge before it resumes its course. From the bridge one can view **a fleet**

of small barges, which we have proposed to be designed by individual artists and outfitted with furnishings for use as floating diners.

An amphitheater stands on a spiral mound near the lake, tangent to the promenade and accessible from the parking area immediately to the north by means of a grand concourse. **The concourse penetrates the mass of the mound,** establishing a place for public facilities and forming a loggia at the intersection with stepped seating areas.

The geometric principles governing the site have much in common with the **scientific and cosmological events** to be celebrated in the proposed natural history museum, and offer a unique opportunity to extend the museum throughout the park via marks and objects representing measurements **in time and space.**

The museum stands at the northern edge of the grove, where its overhanging roof reinforces the circular drive surrounding the grove and frames the northern slopes of the Hollywood Hills in the distance. Beneath the roof, animating the porch that introduces visitors to the park, a glazed canopy suggests the presence of an event from another time, such as the impact of a meteor, while offering a view of the subterranean exhibitions.

The themes developed throughout the site continue in the internal organization of the museum building, which is divided into three vertical layers: a subterranean domain devoted to prehistory, a central volume dedicated to the present and near past, and a technologically sophisticated roof structure assigned to the exploration of the unknown.

VILLA LINDA FLORA,
BEL AIR, CALIFORNIA, PROJECT, 1987

The plan for this forty-acre estate in Pacific Palisades exploits the site's rugged contours to create a choreographic dance of parallax and precipitous slopes. Winding down the spine of the ridge, a line of palms oscillates before the plane of vision, then rotates with the turnabout, treating the visitor to a 360-degree view. A long wall flanked by a shallow stair leads up the hill. One can then glimpse the rounded and sometimes gleaming forms of buildings beyond. At the top, an arbor curves toward a massive portal that frames the long view to the Pacific horizon.

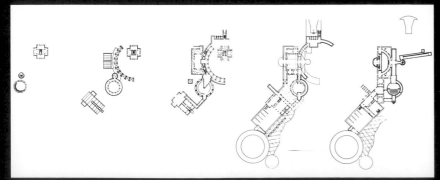

Site plan

LANDSCAPE HAS A CURIOUS ABILITY TO WIN OUR TRUST.
IT IS WHERE WE "ARE." IT IS QUITE LITERALLY ABOVE,
BENEATH, AND AROUND US.
IT IS TRULY "IMMERSIVE," IDENTIFIABLY "REAL."
THIS QUALITY LENDS AUTHORITY TO OUR MORE
CAPRICIOUS IMPULSES AND IMPARTS CREDIBILITY
TO THE OTHERWISE INCOHERENT EVENTS OF
THE EVERYDAY STREETSCAPE.

↑
N

For the visitor, a project such as the Arts Park can provide total immersion in an experience, much as can the now popular virtual reality programs. For an architect, this project affords a rare opportunity to utilize such a synthetic point of view, like that experienced from the Propylaea at the Acropolis, to orchestrate the kinetic and visual experience of individuals within a known area.

Thus, at the Arts Park, one imagines that vehicles on the way to the parking lot, pedestrians embarking at the curb, and children crossing the circular meadow can be choreographed to a high degree. By empathizing with their experience and laying out the terrain with a visual path in mind, we evolved the Arts Park plan from a diagram to a richly textured field of events.

ECOTOPIA, CONCEPTUAL DESIGN, 1982

For a screenplay based on Ernest Callenbach's novel, a tale of an ecologically advanced society, we envisioned a series of mechanisms that capture the aesthetic of an alternative technology.

Bobbing high above San Francisco, a cordon of shimmering balloons pull tight to their tether cables. The arcs of huge propellers emerge as tiny gondolas make their way up to what appear to be cabins. This power plant draws energy from the winds, sending it down the same cables for distribution.

Retrofitted to the wall of an antique mirror-glass office building, a rustic porch signals a New Age presidential suite. Within, hydroponic gardens and high-tech communication systems coexist in harmony.

Giant solar collectors gather electrical energy for storage in huge cylindrical capacitors, where it awaits discharge into magnetic reservoirs that provide acceleration for a high-speed train. An aerodynamic "lifting" fuselage alleviates stress on bridges and trestles, reducing their structure to a surprisingly delicate minimum.

**Sectional axonometric
of cascade**

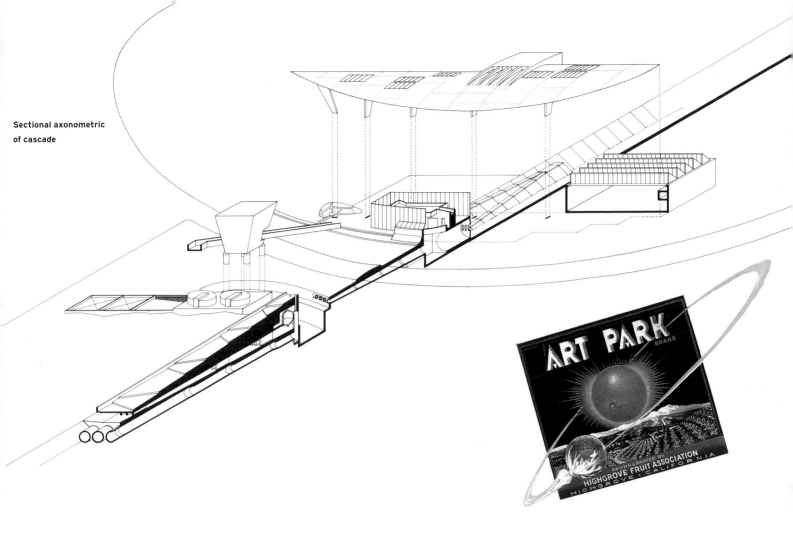

We imagined an outdoor classroom filled with teaching aids, able to communicate the vastness of interplanetary space as well as the infinity of time. One must move not only the eyes but the entire body in order to walk conceptually, for example, from the beginning of time to the time of Christ, while progressing geographically from the center of the circular promenade along a calibrated radius to a destination in time.

THE RIVER AND THE CITY, NICOLLET ISLAND, MINNEAPOLIS, MINNESOTA, 1977

In Minneapolis, a historical core too far removed from the Mississippi riverfront, a dilapidated island, and a deteriorated riverbank beyond offered potential for an urban revival. Walker Art Center director Martin Friedman initiated this study for an exhibition entitled "The River: Images of the Mississippi," asking us to define a possible future for the city's westward expansion.

A new plaza links the core to the shore by cloning Gunnar Birkert's Federal Reserve Bank, creating a linear commercial center and converting an unused rail terminal into a performance hall.

The opposite bank, connected by a signature trolley, offers the office-bound worker an opportunity for a lunch break in a tropical swim palace or a Georgetown-like stroll in a newly created district of townhouses and small shops along an intimate canal.

The east bank features a sweeping riverside boulevard, lined with trees and special work pavilions for a yet-to-be-created Internet sponsored by Minneapolis's corporate Medici.

A new housing quarter for urban singles follows the river, with panoramic views and self-contained shopping and child care.

On the island, a marble Mississippi riverbed rendered at a scale of one foot to one mile invites children and adults to hopscotch with geography. Memorials to Tom Sawyer, Charles Lindbergh, and the city of Memphis mark important points.

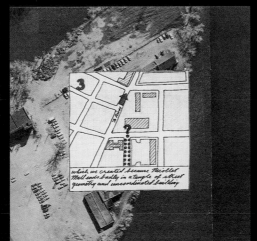

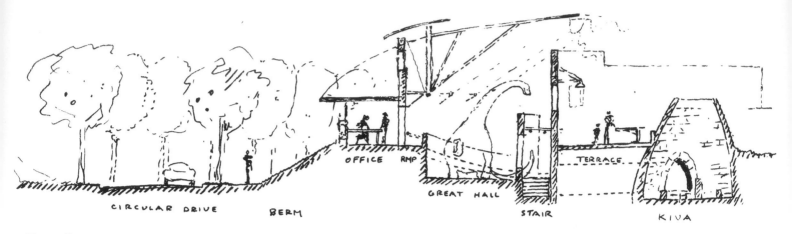

CIRCULAR DRIVE   BERM   OFFICE   RMP   GREAT HALL   STAIR   TERRACE   KIVA

N.H. I

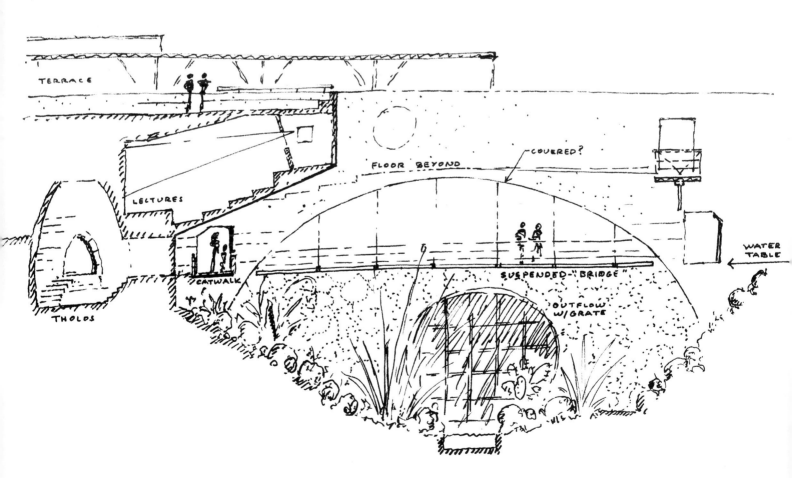

TERRACE   LECTURES   FLOOR BEYOND   COVERED?   WATER TABLE   THOLOS   CATWALK   SUSPENDED "BRIDGE"   OUTFLOW W/ GRATE

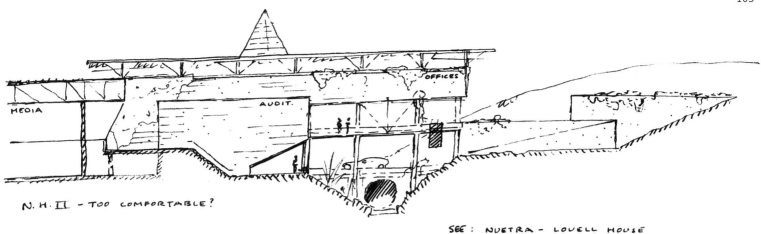

N. H. II - TOO COMFORTABLE?

SEE: NUETRA - LOVELL HOUSE
FLLW - FALLINGWATER

N.H. I

+ BROADCAST SERVICE
OF THE VALLEY ART PARK

+ PUBLIC ACCESS CABLE T.V.

+

MEDIA I

EDIT

EDIT

SOUND
ABSORB

ROLL UP

LUMA
CRANE

TERRACE

VIDEO EDITING

ARCHITECTURE NEED NOT CHALLENGE THOSE TRADITIONS THAT
EXPLICITLY AVOID FORMAL DISCIPLINE.
THE FRONTIER SENSIBILITY RESPONSIBLE FOR MOST CALIFORNIA
BUILDING WAS ONLY OCCASIONALLY SUPERSEDED BY A PRINCIPLED CONCEPTION
(NOTABLY THE WORK OF FRANK LLOYD WRIGHT, RUDOLPH SCHINDLER,
RICHARD NEUTRA, ET AL.). ON THE OTHER HAND, WALT DISNEY
AND ABBOTT KINNEY SAW THE OPPORTUNITY
TO GENERATE FANTASY DOMAINS (ADVENTURELAND, TOMORROWLAND, VENICE)
WHERE OTHERS SAW NOTHING BUT ENDLESS TRACTS.

UCLA GATEWAY, UNIVERSITY OF CALIFORNIA AT LOS ANGELES, 1991

For the Westwood entrance to UCLA, we restructured the relationship of pedestrians, automobile traffic, building mass, and landscape, clarifying the haphazard growth of the campus.

Before: A crisscross of axes and orthogonals hew to vehicular logic, overriding the lawns and paths of the original campus plan.

After: A curving boulevard sweeps through a campus defined by orthogonal paths and broad lawns.

The driver encounters parking kiosks and traffic islands arranged to reinforce the axes and angular shifts introduced by recent haphazard planning.

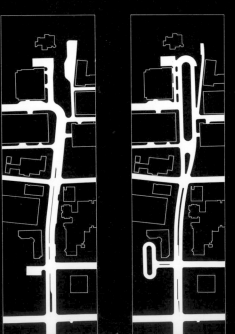

NORMAN BEL GEDDES
AND ÉTIENNE-LOUIS BOULLÉE
MAPPED OUT THE TERRAIN. THEIR WORK DEVELOPS A SCENARIO
THAT EXTENDS BEYOND THE EXPECTATIONS OF THE BRIEF TO ENGAGE THE VISITOR FULLY.
IMAGINE PARTAKING OF GEDDES'S VISION OF A TRANSCONTINENTAL HIGHWAY SYSTEM
AT THE 1939 NEW YORK WORLD'S FAIR FROM THE PERSPECTIVE OF
AN AERIAL FLIGHT ACROSS THE COUNTRY, THEN BEING DEPOSITED AT AN ACTUAL,
FUNCTIONING URBAN INTERCHANGE!

The campus boundary has been extended by physically moving
two 1930s bracket-walls to create a broad lawn.

Conventional entry icons: a flanking wall, stairway, and moat define
a public plaza animated by a kiosk.
The arrangement, however,
suggests shifting priorities and
an ambivalent hierarchy minimally
laced by organizing geometries.

Composite floor plan of museum and media center

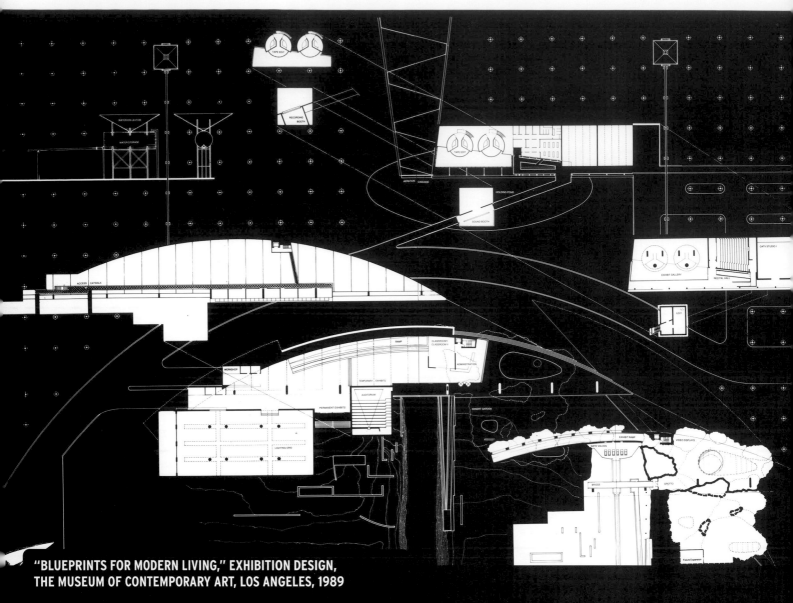

"BLUEPRINTS FOR MODERN LIVING," EXHIBITION DESIGN, THE MUSEUM OF CONTEMPORARY ART, LOS ANGELES, 1989

For this installation at MOCA, we recreated two Case Study houses at full scale within the museum's Temporary Contemporary facility designed by Frank Gehry, allowing for full viewer participation.

Emerging from the central courtyard of the Rapson house, one made a dark ascent to the cantilevered pool of a replica of Pierre Koenig's 1959 Case Study House #22. Below, set against the curve of the cyclorama, a spatial frieze of video monitors featured the memories of Case Study owners, architects, and builders.

The corrugated undersurface of the carport in Ralph Rapson's 1945 Case Study House #4 here defined the entry portico to the exhibition, forcing the visitor to brush past the family jeep just as one might in suburbia circa 1947.

Staying close to the cyclorama, one followed a graphic timeline. Tracing events of the era—the atomic bomb, the ballpoint pen, synthetic fur, a monkey in a capsule—one also traced the sine-wave shape of the wall separating day from night to peer through layers of yellowing sketches at a parade of miniature Case Study houses.

The Temporary Contemporary provided a context for the black aluminum cyclorama that initiated the narrative of "Blueprints for Modern Living" and divided the space into a luminous portrayal of the program's early years and a nighttime environment for its decline.

PROPERTIES
MEDIA VAN
GROTTO

SOUND BOOTH
SOUND EDIT

WATER PURIFICATION

MOBILE MUSEUM MODULE

TOKYO THEME PARK, GATE II MAIN STREET
TOKYO, JAPAN, PROJECT, 1992

This plan for a second gate at a Tokyo theme park provides visitor access to an entertainment zone rather than
to more traditional thrill rides and gated attractions.

At the foot of the Hotel of Horrors and across from the
Drive-By Drive-In, a rusting corrugated fence weaves
uncertainly beneath a freeway. The cracks reveal a neon
jungle within. Directly ahead a concrete mixing plant
throbs with punk music. Laser light tickles its surfaces.
This is "Junk," a dance club roofed by a freeway and lit by
the shards of antique neon signs.

A replica of an arcaded square in Venice, California, glit-
ters with the reflection of tiny lights on the jumping,
humping, cavorting bodies of a dozen low riders–a dystopian version of the Main Street parade. Beyond, a stately
line of palms outlines the path surrounding the lagoon,
a place for a romantic stroll after the blandishments
of the boulevard.

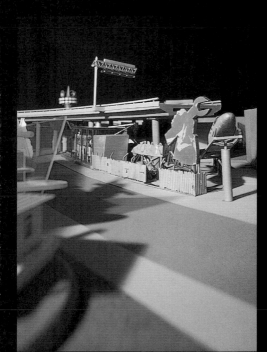

Giant televised real-time images from the Offramp Club
overhead entertain those waiting for the schoolbus/eleva-
tor to descend from its stop atop the freeway and give
them a lift to their dinner tables.

From high on a Ferris wheel the reflections of an anamor-
phic version of the Pacific Design Center play on
a quiet pool.

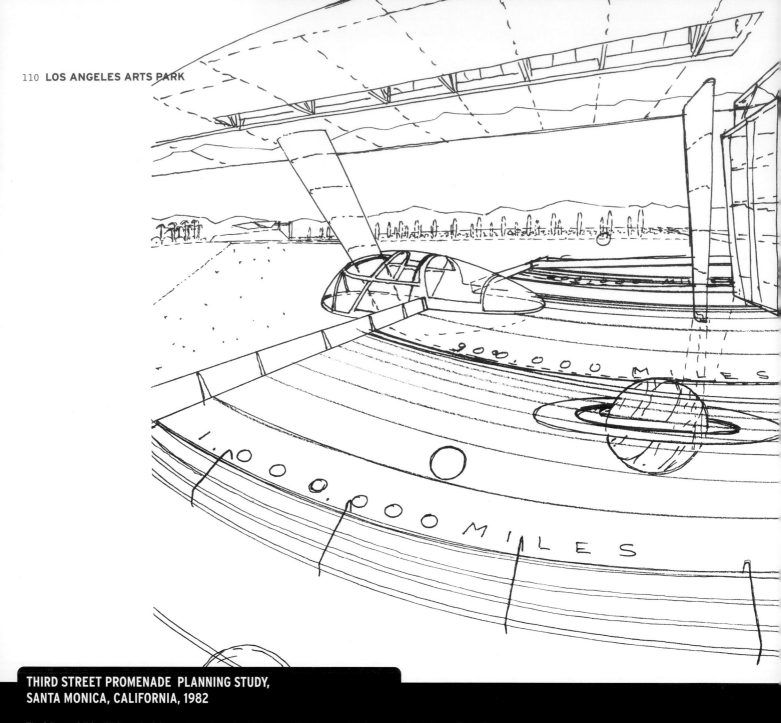

THIRD STREET PROMENADE PLANNING STUDY, SANTA MONICA, CALIFORNIA, 1982

The failure of this 1950s pedestrian mall, contrary to opinion, had little to do with the removal of automobile traffic from the right-of-way and everything to do with the lack of an aggressive identity. Our study concluded that the combination of location, demographics, and vernacular imagery needed only committed management to become a dramatic presence. Design, then, was subordinated to good storytelling.

THIS MORE COMPLEX REALITY
MUST BE ACHIEVED BY
THE IMAGINATIONS OF MANY,
RATHER THAN OF ONE.
THE STORYTELLER,
THE INVENTOR, AND
THE EDITOR MUST COLLABORATE
WITH THE PLUMBER AND
THE ENGINEER.

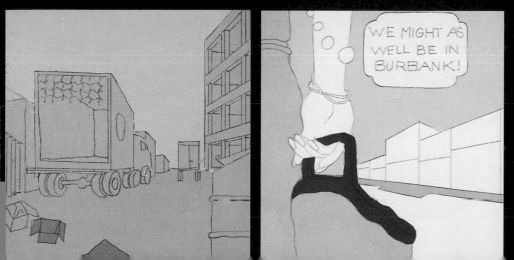

Scientific apparatus and the geometry of scientific theory lent discipline to this site plan: arcs, circles, and trajectories bound by planetary orbits, growth rings, and wave mechanics. The site can be seen as a gigantic system of signs lending order and meaning to an otherwise simple stroll. Landscape elements such as massive spherical stones, gardens, and lines of trees are not mere natural accompaniments but contribute to the overall content.

We differentiate between landscape as plant life and land as the scape of imagination. The unbounded scope of a meaningful order stretching from horizon to horizon is landscape as total composition.

Certain truly great visions, like that of Le Corbusier at Chandigarh, Le Nostre at Chantilly, and the Imperial Palace at Kyoto, exploit this near-perfect synthesis of man-made and the natural, but for most of us there is only a hard-won and always precarious stalemate.

ARCHITECTS SELDOM EXPLOIT THE DRAMATIC OPTIONS CURRENTLY AVAILABLE.
GIVEN THE DIVERSITY OF AVAILABLE MATERIALS, FUNCTIONS, AND LOCATIONS,
MOST DESIGNERS REJECT PLURALISM IN FAVOR OF A NARROW BUT CONTROLLED PALETTE.
HEADS FIRMLY IN THE SAND, THEY DEFEND THE STATUS QUO, IGNORING THE
LIBERATING SPIRIT OF THE AGE.

COMPETITION FOR ROOSEVELT ISLAND, NEW YORK, 1976

Formerly the site of the hog farms that were the garbage collection agency for Manhattan and later of a hospital for the criminally insane, the island enjoys unobstructed views and an uncorrupted identity increasingly rare in the city. We conceived of our entry to this competition for a massive housing project as a means to envision a much-needed prototype for the city's future.

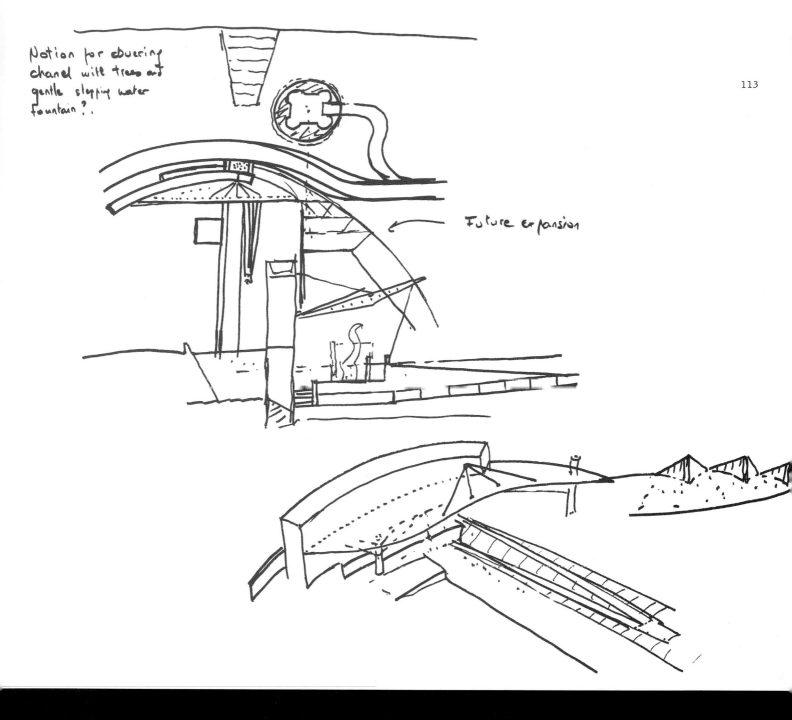

Notion for reducing chanel with trees and gentle stepping water fountain?.

Future expansion

Arriving by bus or car, one encounters the entrance to the housing community, which recalls a medieval plaza, enlivened by the crisscrossing paths of residents and visitors.

A raked sward mortised into the curve of an elevated promenade provides a place for hellos and good-byes, a place for the market and holiday occasions, a place simply to feel the pulse of the community.

A gigantic sow, nurturing her brood, greets residents on their way home, her bronze-green skin growing shiny where she is petted.

At the threshold of the village, as though stepping onto the remains of an aqueduct, one can glimpse narrow passages beyond.

RiversEdge offers a promenade of laundromats, coffee shops, bicycle shops, and child care. A place to read the paper. A site for bicycle races.

A frieze of custom houses visible to Manhattan apartment dwellers crowns the promenade.

The

This Los Angeles headquarters for a
New York-based talent agency
blends the owner's Carnegie Hall style

Imploding Building

with an easy California mix of
inside and outside, stucco and steel, and lush planting.

A transitional neighborhood of tattered bungalows
and new condominiums immediately adjacent to heavily traveled
Santa Monica Boulevard provided a context that we sought to emulate
in the building's massing and materials.

Local zoning ordinances and a problematic site prohibited construction
of a space large enough to accommodate the frenetic activity that
we observed in the New York headquarters. **Dramatic compression
of private areas**—using built-in cabinetry, for instance—
and **virtual elimination** of traditional circulation by exploiting
California's dependably sunny weather helped compensate
for the constricted space.

```
WE NO LONGER RESPOND TO THE STIMULUS OF THE WHOLE.
RATHER, FROM A SHARD WITHOUT CONTEXT,
    WE INTUIT THE WHOLE.
```

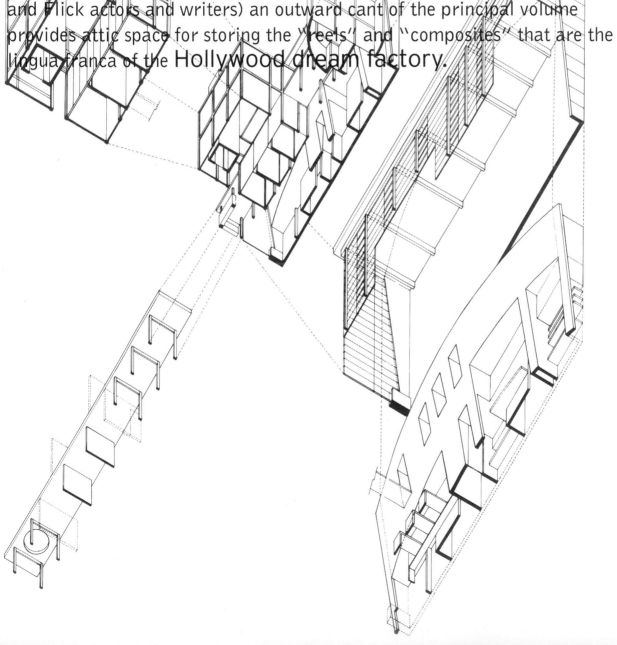

Three contrasting volumes—a gently curved storage/utility cabin, an ovoid conference space, and a cubic open-air lobby—are linked by a simple bridgelike structure and enclosed by a glass wall. This arrangement, especially the contrast between the cell-like voids carved from the mass of larger volumes and the undefined spaces between volumes, provides a range of choice appropriate to the constantly varied protocols of the talent business.

To accommodate the thousands of "virtual" inhabitants (Click models and Flick actors and writers) an outward cant of the principal volume provides attic space for storing the "reels" and "composites" that are the lingua franca of the Hollywood dream factory.

THE CIRCUITRY HERE, AS AN ANALOG OF SURFACE AREA,
ENFOLDS INFORMATION AS A FRACTILE COASTLINE ENFOLDS THE SEA.
VOICES, SCENTS, TRANSACTIONS, AND PLOTS
PERMEATE ITS PORES LIKE WATER IN A SPONGE.

Our fascination with vehicles, cabins, capsules, and appliances gave rise to an architecture in which space and furnishings unite in a single entity. The conventional relationship of space to furnishings could not accommodate the extraordinary size of the staff relative to the space and the operational efficiency required by the client.

However, by focusing on the compressed nature of the agency's activities and adopting formal strategies from naval architecture and the furnishings of long-distance sleeping cars, we were able to combine the minimum footprint of adequate workspace with a greatly expanded "hat" for storage and utilities, creating a set of bunklike workstations inserted in the space's defining volumes.

WE SEEK THE COHERENCE OF COMPATIBILITY,
NOT CONFORMITY, IN A DIVERSE COMMUNITY OF GOOD NATURE.

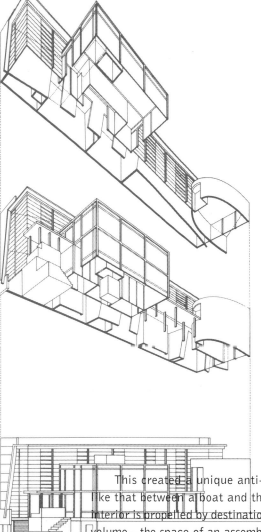

This created a unique anti-space, much like that between a boat and the wharf. The interior is propelled by destination rather than volume—the space of an assembly line rather than an executive office, and one that we had explored earlier in the Pini salon (p. 122) (now destroyed) and in the Cookie Express project (below).

Such a polymorphous architecture creates an environment coded for individual activity rather than group dynamics. Each occupant enjoys a particular space tailored to his or her specific activity. The resulting in-between space is emphatically defined by the bounding "personal" spaces, creating a tribal rather than a corporate environment.

COOKIE EXPRESS, RETAIL PROTOTYPE, 1984

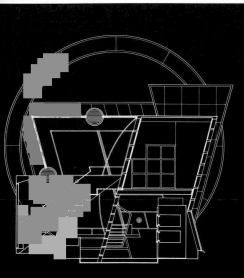

This very small prototype building, with a footprint of only two hundred square feet, contains a full complement of equipment and facilities required for restaurant operation. The business plan anticipated hundreds of these units erected in the parking lots of malls and shopping centers across the country.

A watch must somehow function, though it may occupy no more space than a bottlecap. The design for the Cookie Express employs similar strategies, though it may occupy no more ground space than an automobile.

This typical parking space is occupied by 14,000 pounds of wood, glass, and concrete; two ovens; and a freezer, instead of an automobile's three-hundred horsepower engine, four rubber tires, and two tons of metal and fabric. Each unit can hold up to six people.

Frames built on a jig will lock onto a fiberglass tub as in the Corvette, with mounts and services, wiring harness, and work surfaces.

PINI SALON,
ENCINO, CALIFORNIA, 1987

Specialized furniture elements patterned on
the booths and tunnels of an automobile assembly
plant are here at the service of lacquering,
painting, and trimming the contemporary woman.
Self-referential mechanical shapes for removal
of toxins, hot-air drying, and inspection are
incorporated into a plan in which residual space
loosely structures circulation.

ALCHEMY, UNLIKE TRUE CHEMISTRY,
DEPENDS ON RETENTION OF THE ALLEGORICAL MEANING
OF ITS INGREDIENTS, PURPORTING TO ACHIEVE RESULTS
BY MEANS OF MIXTURE RATHER THAN COMPOUND.

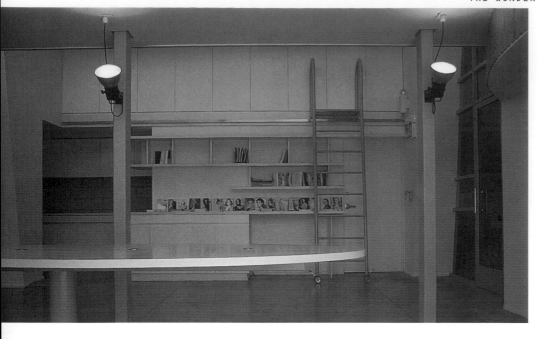

In the Pini Salon, each functional element was configured as a self-contained "processing" space within the larger shell of the mother building. At Click, the self-contained units are wrapped in a thin glass skin for practical reasons only, suggesting minimal protection from the other elements.

This composite architecture, composed of discrete elements and enclosing membranes, is easily assimilated by the typical Los Angeles context. L.A. reads as a casual cluster of forms that might have been erected at roughly the same time. Here even the decaying fence on the adjacent property and the roofs of neighboring buildings are difficult to extricate from the overall domain.

MICROSHOP: INTERACTIVE KIOSK, 1986

Loaded with computers and disk drives and cooled by a pair of squirrel-cage fans, the Microshop kiosk was to proliferate in bookshops and arcades. Users would select merchandise, schedule trips, or purchase tickets by interacting with demos and promos stocked by the participating brands, thus reducing the footprint of a "virtual shopping center" to less than a yard.

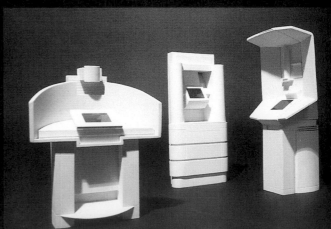

VILLA LINDA FLORA,
BEL AIR, CALIFORNIA, PROJECT, 1987

The visual resemblance between an architecture of geometry and transition and the moving parts of a mechanical device stems from the candor that disciplines the design of each.

The complexities of site and occupation yield to axes and descriptive geometry.

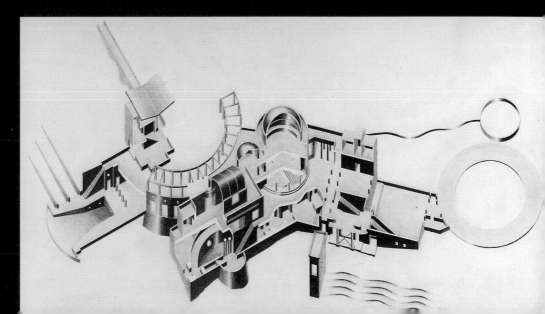

THE COMPRESSIVE FORCES EXERTED BY THE CONTAINING WALLS
OF A MEDIEVAL CITY DISTORT THE OTHERWISE PLATONIC FORMS OF SIMPLE
CONTAINERS MUCH AS A TRASH COMPACTOR DISTORTS SODA CANS, CEREAL BOXES,
AND SOUP TINS.

All architecture, of course, can only be seen in context, and thus, to the degree that context is subject to change, the visual meaning of architecture will follow suit. The monumental, with its commitment to singularity and implied hierarchy, is rapidly becoming an anachronism, especially on the Internet. The cultural evolution of art, literature, music, dance, and even film (CD-ROM, the Sega video game) seems inexorably biased toward the open-ended, the flexible, or the intermediate. In a society rich in the transfer of information, the role of architecture in cultural dialogue is unfortunately fixed in both place and form. It is precisely the nature of buildings as permanent and inflexible that often makes architects unwitting co-conspirators with the more reactionary elements of society.

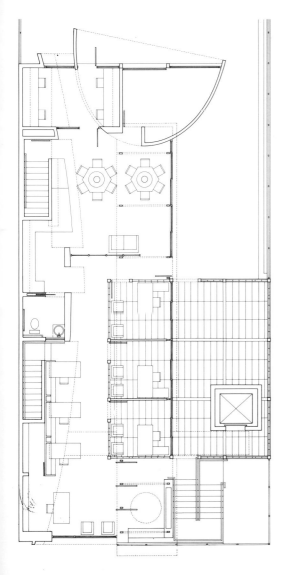

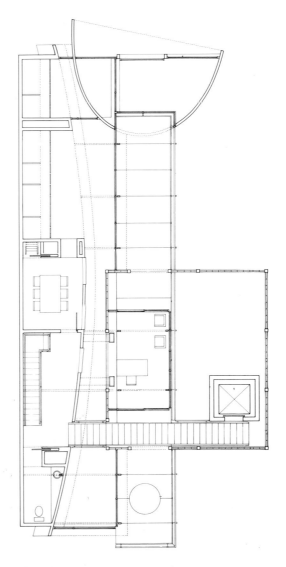

Second level plan

Mezzanine level plan

SOMETIMES WE CAN (GRATEFULLY) FIND OUR WAY WITHOUT A SIGN.

Buildings that reinforce monumentality and autonomy run the risk of asserting values long since consigned to the scrap heap. Yet because the context modifies our perception of supposedly autonomous objects, monumentality itself is no guarantee of "meaning."

The perception of space depends on articulation of defining elements. This is independent of the nature of the space, whether Euclidian, chaotic, or fractile. When the defining elements are seen as a "set" and cohere as abstract planes, markers, or boundaries without symbolic or mnemonic context, we perceive a "space" as opposed to a "place." The walled enclosure of the typical European plaza is a place; the bounded "virtual" definition of Larry Bell's sculptural cubes creates a space. But a successful antispace consciously avoids the generating references necessary to form a coherent visualization. It is thus dynamic, energetic, and unexpected.

UCLA required this temporary building

Built-in Life Cycle: All

to house the collections of the main undergraduate library
while the original library undergoes seismic renovation.

A group of fabric tension structures, one for administration
and three for the collection and reading rooms,
receives an extension of the original campus axis and redirects it
toward the active student center to the south. A recessed courtyard
at the beginning of Janss Steps offers a site for socializing.
An existing monumental balustrade terminates the axis
and initiates the internal axes and radii governing the design.

THE NEW REALITY IS DEFINED BY DISTRIBUTION, WHETHER OF GOODS OR IDEAS.
SATELLITE BROADCASTS, CONTAINER SHIPS, AND TRADEMARKS BLANKET THE PLANET
WITH AVIS, BENETTON, APPLE, AND HYUNDAI LOGOS,
LIKE SO MANY BOTANICAL SPECIES. THE PARALLEL IS OBVIOUS:
THE FRUIT OF THE EARTH, ONCE THE SOLE SOURCE OF CRAFTS, ARTS, AND COMMERCE,
HAS A SYNTHETIC COMPETITOR FROM WHICH WE PICK TRANSISTORS,
ENTERTAINMENTS, AND CONVENIENCES LIKE FRUITS FROM A TREE.
THIS NEW EQUATION SUGGESTS THAT
PERMANENCE MUST COMPETE WITH THE EPHEMERAL
FOR MEANING AND VALUE.

Buildings are Temporary

The **primary tensile structure,** in the form of a sloping shed, houses the library stacks and other student services. A **five-eighths cylindrical tube** contains administrative offices. There are **two reading rooms,** one circular in plan and one semicircular. An intentionally varied ensemble of disposable wood, masonry, and plastic substructures provides for special conditions, sometimes suggesting the foundations of a building no longer present— thus reinforcing by contrast the temporary nature of the structure that covers it.

↑
N

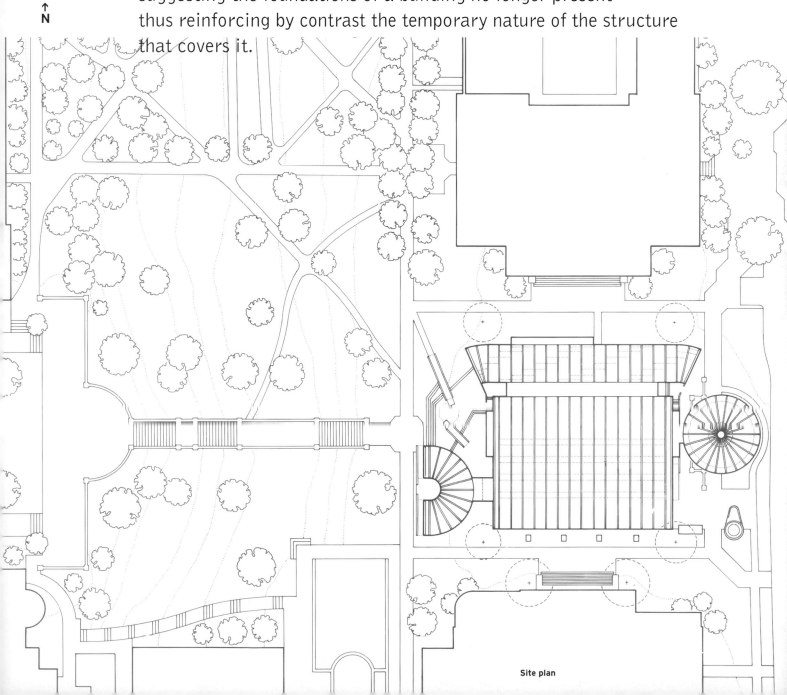

Site plan

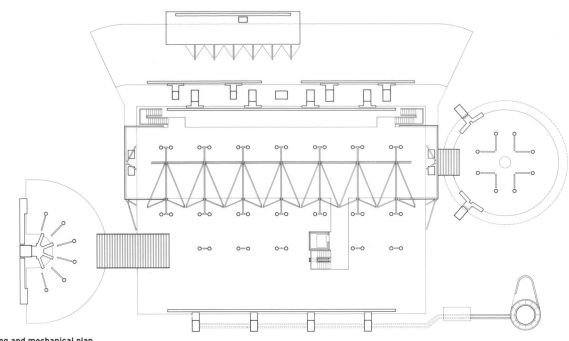

Lighting and mechanical plan

AS STRUCTURE APPROACHES THE LIGHTNESS OF THE ZEPPELIN,
        THERE ARE FEW PRACTICAL BARRIERS TO AN ARCHITECTURE CONCEIVED AS FURNITURE.
WHY NOT PROVIDE EXTENSIONS TO THE BUILDING PROPER THAT ARE THEMSELVES USEFUL?

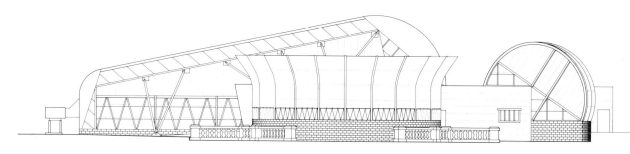

West elevation

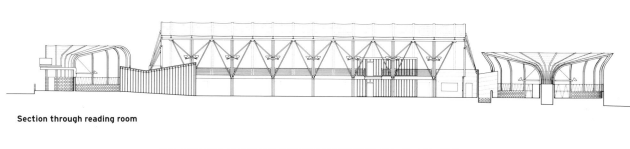

Section through reading room

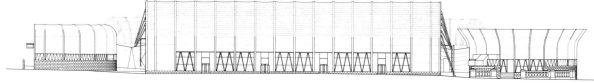

North elevation

A **prefabricated steel mezzanine** stretches the length of the
building, supported by paired steel-tube columns. One side extends
vertically to follow the axis established by James Stern.
Clipped to and stabilized by the columns are the aluminum bents
of the roof structure itself, which are received by a masonry utility core.
Braced end walls cantilever to within a few feet of the roof
structure, from which sliding planes of thermoplastic complete
the enclosure yet allow for the twenty-eight inches of horizontal movement
anticipated during high winds.

In keeping with the temporary nature of the structure, all materials and assembly details were optimized to minimize cost and complexity. As in an aircraft, decorative emphasis lies in the orchestration of fasteners, cables, and exposed elements necessary for efficient operation. Even the colors of the fabric skin have an impact on energy consumption.

The off-the-shelf materials, combined with the novel nature of the main structure, had an unexpected dividend, blurring hard-and-fast trade boundaries and encouraging cooperation among construction workers.

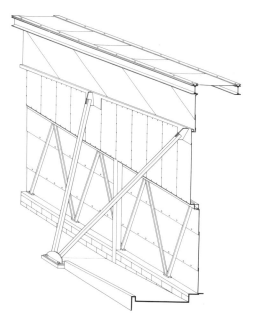

Wall bracing detail

All buildings are temporary: all have some sort of life cycle and reflect the technology, customs, and economics of the times. Buildings are also linked in a continuum of material evolution and accommodation to change. Yet a building rarely reflects its time as clearly as do film and music. Buildings straddle periods, relating to evolving futures while swimming in the wake of the past.

Towell allowed us to connect more directly with right now, due to the immediate need for the structure and its relatively short life cycle. We deemed experimentation with materials and methods appropriate as long as they met cost objectives and performance goals. We confronted materials, fasteners, and geometry from the perspective of first-time use, discarding tradition a priori.

MODERN TECHNOLOGY, FOR ALL ITS PRAGMATIC CONSTRAINTS,
OFFERS A VAST AND MYSTERIOUS TERRAIN NEARLY AS ELUSIVE AS THAT OF A RAIN FOREST.
IS IT ANY WONDER THAT THERE ARE THOSE AMONG US WHO WOULD CREATE A THEOLOGY
BUILT UPON THEIR REVELATIONS? ARCHITECTS, WHO ARE NO LONGER
PARTICULARLY WELL SUITED TO THEIR PERCEIVED ROLE AS CULTURAL INTERPRETERS,
MUST NEVERTHELESS STRUGGLE TO INCORPORATE A SEMBLANCE OF TECHNICAL UNDERSTANDING
IN THEIR PROJECTS OR RISK SEEMING HOPELESSLY ARCANE.
ONE CANNOT HELP BUT REFLECT THAT SUCH EFFORTS, LIKE THE "SPEED LINES" ON MODERN APPLIANCES,
DO NOTHING SO MUCH AS REVEAL THE DESIGNER'S LACK OF TRUE INSIGHT.

GEOMETRY CONFERS BEING WITHOUT REGARD FOR WEIGHT
OR SUBSTANCE. A NET OF PURE LINES CAN DESCRIBE VOLUMES THAT WE CAN EASILY TRAVERSE
WITHOUT PHYSICAL MOVEMENT. IN AN ARCHITECTURE WITHOUT SUBSTANCE,
INFINITELY RESONANT BOUNDARIES CONTAIN ONLY THE ACTIVITES OF THE MOMENT.

The physical constraints embodied in the form of many mechanical devices—not only cars and aircraft engines—offer a metaphor for the activity, density, stress, and spatial relationships that must be considered in the design of a building. These relationships are for the most part untainted by the hierarchy, symbolism, and materialism that still cling to the practice of architecture.

Unlike the reductive architectural implications of a contest between form and function, the design of mechanical components is devoted to the unwavering search for performance. The degree of physical stress, combined with an absolute requirement for efficiency, leads to a vocabulary of machine forms in which space, volume, and strength are carefully apportioned according to need. This generates a commensurate poetry of ribs, radii, and fillets directly related to the confluence of purpose and constraints. Our architecture stands to the heroic purity of such forms as a compromised but loyal follower.

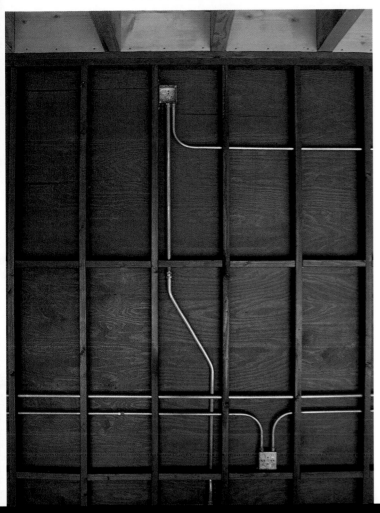

DOMORE SHOWROOM, 1988

The Domore Furniture Corporation asked us to create a novel "event" to announce its presence at Westweek, Los Angeles's annual designer's trade fair. For this most ephemeral of architectural expressions, we designed an invitation in the form of a transparent red-and-blue viewer that "reconstructed" a flat, two-dimensional building facade into a three-dimensional reality.

Admittedly hampered by cost and convention, we seek to avoid the pitfall of visual imagery and adopt instead the principles of design observed in technological triumphs. For example, Erich Mendelsohn's Einstein Tower is a "romantic" emulation of technology that seriously compromises the integrity of its brick structure in the service of an image, while James Stirling's Leicester laboratory uses materials and techniques without compromise to "reveal" a compelling reality. Mendelsohn swore never to build again in so cumbersome a manner while Stirling produced a remarkable series of buildings, each of which amplifies and builds upon the vocabulary established by the laboratory.

Our own fascination with mobility and architecture dates from the 1970s, when the space program, The Whole Earth Catalogue, and the rise of alternative politics and lifestyles demanded an architecture of improvisation based on egalitarian principles. Our project for a mobile theater, called 00:00, reflects the idealism of that moment, and the digital readout implied by its name suggests rapid erection and deployment. Projects for an integrated transportation system and a factory-produced housing system (which evolved into the Franklin/La Brea project nearly twenty years later) reflect our interest in the practical realization of those same goals in an urban design framework.

ZIP CHIP TECHNOLOGY, 1987

For Applefest, an annual trade fair for computer devotees, we created this Apple "juice bar" for the manufacturer of the ZIP high-speed computer chip (which was able to accelerate the speed of a standard Macintosh computer). The jukeboxlike counter elements demonstrated the component in use while an overhead clock portrayed the "accelerated" rate of operation.

"THE MAGIC OF PLAY," EXHIBITION DESIGN, GEORGIO BEVERLY HILLS, 1994

The need for self-contained, diffused lighting for a temporary exhibition of photography suggested the high-wire trestles that form the backbone of this installation. Acting as a three-hinged arch, the spiderweight wire structure integrates with luminous panels, halogen lighting, and display surfaces to form a complete display system.

Installation view: parallel spaces developed by three-hinged arch system. A weighted base with a friction sole develops the necessary friction to oppose horizontal forces.

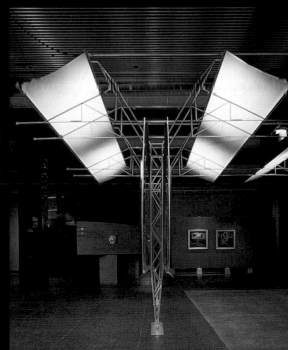

Installation view: wire trestle and aluminum panel.

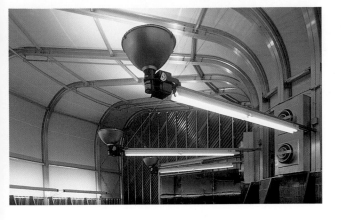

Exploded axonometric

Archigram's radical premise that the components of cities might someday be clipped together, "plugged in," and rearranged at will, visually expresses the dynamic of urban change. Now, as lightweight structures and electronic systems liberate architecture from the economic bonds of land speculation and capital investment, one can house functions once considered inseparable from monumental imagery in structures that are gay, spontaneous, and short-lived. Moving components, Archigram-style, are the most dramatic means to achieve flexibility, but in a full-scale architectural context also the most complex and costly. It is hard to justify a major investment in movable infrastructure or connections on a "what if" basis of change (witness the movable floors at the Pompidou.

Towell was designed as a facility for serial reuse and relocation on the UCLA campus (everything from dance space to retail shops will follow its use as a library); thus we configured the building as a set of fixed but programmatically discrete parts. One need not move anything to reprogram its use, but parts can be shifted elsewhere on campus as required.

Frank Gehry, James Stirling, Alvar Aalto, Le Corbusier, the Wright brothers, Eiffel, McCormick, Paxton: a new breed of designers seized upon the pragmatic principles of the Industrial Revolution to govern the construction of buildings. By divesting their work of traditional "architectural" content yet remaining faithful to abiding principles of human scale and emotion, they invented a compelling architecture.

Towell continues this tradition by harnessing materials to the physical attributes of referential space, creating a multivalent space in which the defining elements are the boxes of air-handling units, the braces for roofing ribs, the ballast boxes of fluorescent lamps, and the regular rhythm of the sprinkler system.

OFTEN PROJECTS OF AMBITIOUS SCOPE BUT LIMITED MEANS
MUST AVAIL THEMSELVES OF INGENIOUS SOLUTIONS,
NO MATTER WHAT THE PRECEDENTS OR AESTHETIC CONSEQUENCES.
SINCE MANY OF OUR PROJECTS FALL INTO THIS CATEGORY, WE HAVE FOUND
THAT NO SYSTEM OF PRIORITIES CAN REPLACE
A CONTINUOUS AND SINCERE EMPATHY FOR THE USER.

00:00, A MOBILE THEATER, PROTOTYPE, 1972

A touring company of the musical <u>Hair</u> commissioned this
design for a theater capable of rapid deployment to a
string of parks and playgrounds across the country.

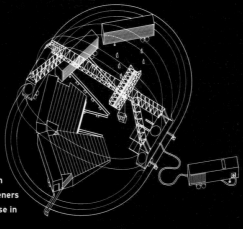

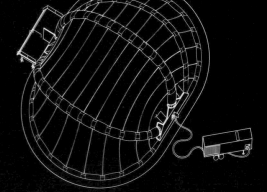

A structure formed by a reinforced fabric
tube filled with high-pressure air is borne by two semitrailers
containing mobile blowers. A double-membrane skin
provides acoustical and temperature control. Lacing and fasteners
in contrasting colors articulate the surface much like those in
antique Japanese armor.

Routine inflation and disassembly suggested that the components of the theater nest and travel
in a concise form. The basic seating and lighting array is contained within a group of four trailers,
which can be arranged in a variety of configurations within the envelope.

A gantry bridge supporting lighting and a control booth can be positioned as desired within the space
and moved during performance. It also acts as a fail-safe structure in the event of a pressure and/or power failure.

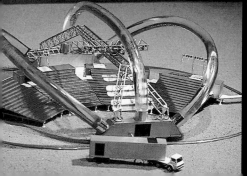

List of Projects

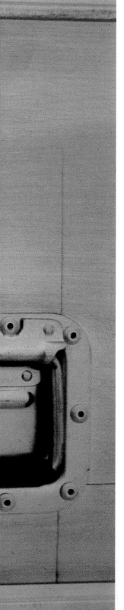

Architectural Projects

AMERICAN CINEMATHEQUE
Hollywood, California, 1995–
CLIENT: American Cinematheque
DESIGN TEAM: Eric Holmquist, Andrew Lindley, Michael Swischuk
CONSULTANTS: Englekirk & Sabol Consulting Engineers, Inc. (structural), Boston Light & Sound (projection & sound), Mekay Conant Brook (acoustics)

SAN FRANCISCO ART INSTITUTE GRADUATE STUDENT CENTER
San Francisco, 1995–
CLIENT: San Francisco Art Institute
DESIGN TEAM: Yanan Par, Shawn Sullivan
CONSULTANT: Ove Arup & Partners (structural, mechanical, electrical)

OCCIDENTAL COLLEGE SCULPTURE STUDIO
Los Angeles, 1994–
CLIENT: Occidental College
ASSOCIATE ARCHITECT: Levin & Associates
DESIGN TEAM: Yanan Par, David Campbell,
CONSULTANTS: Babsco Enterprises (electrical), Englekirk & Sabol Consulting Engineers, Inc. (structural), The Sullivan Partnership (mechanical)

MEDIA CENTER AND NATURAL HISTORY MUSEUM
(invited competition)
Sepulveda Basin, Los Angeles, 1989–
CLIENT: The Cultural Foundation
DESIGN TEAM: Frank Clementi, Julie Smith, Michael Swischuk

CRAFT AND FOLK ART MUSEUM
Los Angeles, 1995
CLIENT: Craft and Folk Art Museum
DESIGN TEAM: Lynn Batsch, Eric Holmquist, Peter Noble, Yanan Par, Shawn Sullivan
CONSULTANTS: Mel Bilow & Associates (mechanical), Patrick Byrne & Associates (electrical), Mike Ishler, Parker Resnick (structural)
CONTRACTOR: Van Holland Construction Co.

ENVIRONMENTAL HEALTH AND SAFETY FACILITY
Los Angeles, 1995
CLIENT: University of California at Los Angeles
DESIGN TEAM: Eric Holmquist
CONSULTANTS: Patrick Byrne and Associates (electrical), Englekirk & Sabol Consulting Engineers, Inc. (structural), Rosenberg and Associates (mechanical)

LORD DENTSU & PARTNERS ADVERTISING AGENCY
Los Angeles, 1995
CLIENT: Lord Dentsu & Partners
DESIGN TEAM: Mark Kruger, Yanan Par, Shawn Sullivan, Selwyn Ting
CONSULTANTS: Patrick Byrne and Associates (electrical), Bruce Resnick (structural), The Sullivan Partnership (mechanical)

MOBILIZED ASSISTANCE SHELTER FOR THE HOMELESS, CRISIS INTERVENTION CENTER
(invited competition)
Las Vegas, Nevada, 1994
CLIENT: City of Las Vegas
DESIGN TEAM: Lynn Batsch, Eric Holmquist, Peter Noble, Yanan Par, Stevens Wilson
ASSOCIATE ARCHITECT: Lucchesi, Galati Architects

CLICK & FLICK AGENCY
West Hollywood, California, 1992
CLIENT: Click Model Management & the Flick Talent Agency
DESIGN TEAM: Lynn Batsch, Frank Clementi
CONSULTANTS: Patrick Byrne (electrical), Interstate Mechanical Systems (mechanical), Niver Engineering (structural)
CONTRACTOR: Pacific Southwest Development, Inc.

TOWELL LIBRARY
University of California at Los Angeles, 1992
CLIENT: UCLA Capital Programs
DESIGN TEAM: Robert Flock, Peter Noble
CONSULTANTS: Patrick Byrne & Associates (electrical), Robert Englekirk Engineering, Inc. (structural), A. C. Martin & Associates (civil); Rubb Inc. (shell), The Sullivan Partnership (mechanical)
CONTRACTOR: American Constructors California, Inc.

HEMDALE FILM CORPORATION AND OFFICE FACILITY
Los Angeles, 1990
CLIENT: Hemdale Film Corporation
DESIGN TEAM: Bill Molthen, John Trautmann, Rachel Vert
CONSULTANTS: Robert Lawson (structural), Nikolapokus & Associates (electrical), The Sullivan Partnership, Inc. (mechanical)
CONTRACTOR: Pacific Southwest Development, Inc.

WEST HOLLYWOOD CIVIC CENTER
(competition)
West Hollywood, California, 1989
CLIENT: City of West Hollywood
DESIGN TEAM: Frank Clementi

FRANKLIN/LA BREA HOUSING
(invited competition)
Hollywood, California, 1988
CLIENT: Los Angeles Community Redevelopment
Agency / The Museum of Contemporary Art
DESIGN TEAM: Aaron Betsky, Frank Clementi
CONSULTANT: Ove Arup & Partners (structural,
mechanical, electrical)

**COMPOSITE IMAGE SYSTEMS POST
PRODUCTION FACILITY**
Hollywood, California, 1987
CLIENT: Joe Matza
DESIGN TEAM: John Trautmann, Mary Weather Felt

PINI SALON
Encino, California, 1987
CLIENT: Jonathan Pini
DESIGN TEAM: Kevin Daly, Rachel Vert
CONSULTANT: Niver Engineering (structural)
CONTRACTOR: Rotondi Construction

PNINI MEDICAL OFFICES
Beverly Hills, California, 1986
CLIENT: Alon Pnini
DESIGN TEAM: Kevin Daly, Rachel Vert
CONTRACTOR: Frank Martin

**SEOUL SUMMER OLYMPICS ATHLETES' AND
REPORTERS' VILLAGE**
(invited competition)
Seoul, Korea, 1985
CLIENT: Olympic Organizing Committee
ASSOCIATE ARCHITECT: Charles Kober
and Associates

COOKIE EXPRESS
(Retail Prototype), 1984
CLIENT: Jonathan Baker

SOUTHSIDE SETTLEMENT COMMUNITY CENTER
Columbus, Ohio, 1980
CLIENT: Barbara Stovall, Director
DESIGN PARTNER: Robert Mangurian
DESIGN TEAM: Marianne Burkhalter, Frank Lupo,
Audrey Matlock, Thane Roberts
ASSOCIATE ARCHITECT: Feinknopf,
Macioce & Schappa, Columbus
CONSULTANTS: Geiger Berger (structural),
David Tritt (community liason)
CONTRACTOR: The Gardner Co.

CREATIVE PLAYTHINGS RETAIL SHOP
New York, 1969
CLIENT: Creative Playthings
DESIGN PARTNERS: Keith Godard (graphic
design), Robert Mangurian, Lester Walker
CONSULTANTS: Jules Fisher (lighting),
Morton Subotnik (music composition)

Urban Design Projects

VESEY PLACE
(invited competition)
Battery Park City, New York, 1994
CLIENT: Battery Park City Authority
DESIGN TEAM: Michael Swischuk, Selwyn Ting

**HUDSON WILCOX MIXED-USE
DEVELOPMENT**
Hollywood, California, 1992
CLIENT: Los Angeles Community
Redevelopment Agency
DESIGN TEAM: Peter Noble

UCLA GATEWAY
Los Angeles, 1991
CLIENT: University of California at Los Angeles
DESIGN TEAM: Pier Luigi Montanini, John
Trautmann, Rachel Vert
ASSOCIATE ARCHITECT: Meyer & Allen
Associates, Los Angeles
CONSULTANTS: Hayakawa Associates Consulting
Engineers (electrical), Kennedy/Jenks/Chilton (civil),
Robert Lawson Structural Engineers (structural)
CONTRACTOR: Park Construction

LOS ANGELES ARTS PARK
(invited competition)
Sepulveda Basin, Los Angeles, 1989
CLIENT: The Cultural Foundation, Los Angeles
DESIGN PARTNERS: Mary Miss, Adèle Naudé
Santos, Charles Pearson, Mark Rios
DESIGN TEAM: Frank Clementi, Bruce Prescott

VENICE INTERARTS CENTER
Venice, California, 1983
CLIENT: Beyond Baroque Foundation; Social and
Public Arts Resource Center (SPARC);
LA Theater Works
DESIGN PARTNER: Robert Mangurian
DESIGN TEAM: Kent Hodgetts, Lisa Johnson
& Patty Owen Associates, Heather Kurze,
Dan Rhodes, Katie Spitz

THIRD STREET PROMENADE PLANNING STUDY
Santa Monica, California, 1982
CLIENT: Santa Monica Chamber of Commerce
DESIGN PARTNER: Robert Mangurian
DESIGN TEAM: Sarah Meeker

THE RIVER AND THE CITY
Nicollet Island, Minneapolis, Minnesota, 1976
CLIENT: The Walker Art Center
DESIGN PARTNER: Robert Mangurian
DESIGN TEAM: Audrey Matlock, Thane Roberts,
Caryn Robins

ROOSEVELT ISLAND
(invited competition)
New York, 1976
CLIENT: City of New York
DESIGN PARTNER: Robert Mangurian

LITTLE TOKYO URBAN DESIGN
Los Angeles, 1975
CLIENT: Los Angeles Community Redevelopment
Agency/The Museum of Contemporary Art
DESIGN TEAM: Blake Hodgetts

Entertainment Design

EXPANSION PLAN FOR THE UNIVERSAL AMPHITHEATER
(invited competition)
Universal City, California, 1995
CLIENT: MCA Development Company
DESIGN TEAM: Mark Kruger, Selwyn Ting,
Stevens Wilson

DEEP ROCK DRIVE
1994
CLIENT: Deep Rock Drive, Inc.
DESIGN TEAM: Yanan Par
CONSULTANT: Unleashed (graphics)

PEPSI CITY WORKS
1994
CLIENT: Berman•Katz
DESIGN TEAM: Yanan Par

SONY FORUM
Berlin, Germany, 1994
CLIENT: Robert Fitzpatrick Consultants
DESIGN TEAM: Peter Noble, Yanan Par
CONSULTANT: Unleashed (graphics)

CITYWALK SIGNAGE
Universal City, California, 1993
CLIENT: MCA Development Company
DESIGN COLLABORATOR: Charles White III
DESIGN TEAM: Bob Bangham

PANASONIC PAVILION
Universal City, California, 1993
CLIENT: MCA Development Company
PROJECT MANAGER: Lynn Batsch
DESIGN TEAM: Kent Hodgetts, Peter Noble,
Michael Swischuk
CONSULTANT: Daniel, Mann, Johnson
& Mendenhall (electrical and structural),
Tom Hartman (graphics)
CONTRACTOR: Pacific Southwest Development Inc.

STARSHIP
Las Vegas, Nevada, 1993
CLIENT: Bally's Casino Resort
DESIGN TEAM: Kent Hodgetts, Peter Noble
CONSULTANT: Tom Hartman (graphics)

TOKYO GATE II MAIN STREET
Tokyo, Japan, 1992
CLIENT: Walt Disney Imagineering
DESIGN COLLABORATOR: Charles White III
DESIGN TEAM: Bob Bangham, Alec Kobayashi,
Michael Swischuk

ROCKPLEX ENTERTAINMENT CENTER
Universal City, California, 1990
CLIENT: MCA Development Company
DESIGN COLLABORATOR: Charles White III

00:00, A MOBILE THEATER
(prototype)
1972
CLIENT: Michael Butler (Berkshire, England),
Jules Fisher (New York)
DESIGN TEAM: Peter de Bretteville, Eugene Kupper

Residential Projects

VISO HOUSE
Hollywood, California, 1990
CLIENT: John Benardello
DESIGN TEAM: Frank Clementi
CONSULTANTS: Gordon Polon (structural),
Grover and Associates (geotechnical)
CONTRACTOR: Dennis Bailey

SCHRAGE/BUTLER HOUSE
Santa Monica, California, 1989
CLIENT: Robert Schrage and Sheri Butler
DESIGN TEAM: Frank Clementi, Julie Smith
CONSULTANT: Niver Engineering
CONTRACTOR: R & M Construction

GOETZ HOUSE
Studio City, California, 1988
CLIENT: Theodore and Sandra Goetz
DESIGN TEAM: David Van Handel, Rachel Vert
CONSULTANT: Niver Engineering
CONTRACTOR: Golden Hammer

VILLA LINDA FLORA
Bel Air, California, 1987
CLIENT: Dan Buchner
DESIGN TEAM: David Van Handel, Rachel Vert

CORMAN HOUSE
Brentwood, California, 1985
CLIENT: Roger and Julie Corman
CONSULTANT: Ken Niver Associates (structural)
CONTRACTOR: Beach Dickerson

GAGOSIAN HOUSE AND GALLERY
Venice, California, 1979
CLIENT: Larry Gagosian
DESIGN PARTNER: Robert Mangurian
DESIGN TEAM: Frank Lupo, Audrey Matlock
CONSULTANTS: Ismail & Wagner (structural),
The Sullivan Partnership (mechanical)
CONTRACTOR: F & G Construction

Exhibition Design

**CALIFORNIA STATE ARCHIVES MUSEUM
PERMANENT EXHIBIT**
Sacramento, California, 1997
CLIENT: California State Archives
COLLABORATOR: Tom Hartman
DESIGN TEAM: Christine Cho, Ken Mattiuz,
Douglas Pierson
CONSULTANTS: Cammisa & WIPF (electrical),
Guttman & Macritche (mechanical), Rutherford
& Chekene (structural)

THROUGH THEIR EYES: CHARLES AND RAY EAMES
(working title)
Traveling Exhibition, 1997
CLIENT: Vitra Design Museum
DESIGN TEAM: Yanan Par, Douglas Pierson
PROJECT DIRECTOR: Donald Albrecht
CONSULTANT: Eames Dimitrious (video)

ART AND FILM
Los Angeles, 1996
CLIENT: The Museum of Contemporary Art,
Los Angeles
DESIGN TEAM: Michael Swischuck, Selwyn Ting
CONSULTANT: Peter Kirby (video)
CURATOR: Kerry Brougher
INSTALLATION: John Bowsher

EXPERIENCE MUSIC PROJECT
Seattle, Washington, 1995–
CLIENT: Experience Music Project
DESIGN TEAM: Mark Kruger, Ken Mattiuz,
Douglas Pierson, Selwyn Ting

SUN POWER
Bad Oeynhausen, Germany, 1995
CLIENT: Dr. Manfred Ragati, Elecktrizitätswerk
Minden-Ravensberg GmbH
DESIGN TEAM: Ken Mattiuz, Stevens Wilson
CONSULTANTS: Jon Biondo (electronics),
Blake Hodgetts (music composition)
FABRICATOR: Serrurier Associates

THE MAGIC OF PLAY
New York, 1995
CLIENT: Giorgio Beverly Hills
DESIGN TEAM: Eric Holmquist, Michael Swischuk
CURATOR: Diana Edkins
INSTALLATION: Face Fabrication & Architecture

THE MAGIC OF PLAY
Los Angeles, 1994
CLIENT: Giorgio Beverly Hills
DESIGN TEAM: Eric Holmquist, Mark Kruger
CURATOR: Diana Edkins
INSTALLATION: Serrurier Associates

FLIGHTS OF FANCY
Los Angeles, 1994
CLIENT: Pacific Design Center, *I.D.: The International
Design Magazine*
DESIGN TEAM: Jennifer Siegal, Stevens Wilson
CURATORS: Gerry Kavanaugh, Michael McDonough
INSTALLATION: Hodgetts + Fung

WINGS OF CHANGE
Los Angeles, 1993
CLIENT: Giorgio Beverly Hills, Director's
Guild of America
DESIGN TEAM: Michael Swischuk
CURATOR: Diane Edkins
INSTALLATION: Serrurier Associates

AST COMPUTERS
COMDEK trade show, Las Vegas, Nevada, 1992
CLIENT: AST Computers
DESIGN COLLABORATOR: Charles White III
DESIGN TEAM: Cam Deleon, Frank Clementi

CALIFORNIA, THE CULTURAL EDGE
Los Angeles, 1992
CLIENT: Giorgio Beverly Hills, Director's
Guild of America
DESIGN TEAM: Tom Hartman, Kent Hodgetts,
Michael Swischuk
INSTALLATION: Serrurier Associates

**BLUEPRINTS FOR MODERN LIVING: HISTORY AND
LEGACY OF THE CASE STUDY HOUSES**
The Temporary Contemporary, The Museum of
Contemporary Art, Los Angeles, 1989
CLIENT: The Museum of Contemporary Art,
Los Angeles
DESIGN TEAM: Frank Clementi, Silja Tilner
CURATOR: Elizabeth A.T. Smith
CONSULTANTS: Peter Kirby (video), David & Sandy
Wasco (prop and artifact)
INSTALLATION: John Bowsher

DOMORE SHOWROOM
Los Angeles, 1988
CLIENT: Westweek, Pacific Design Center
DESIGN TEAM: Aaron Betsky, Frank Clementi,
Julie Smith
GRAPHIC PRODUCTION: Metro Media
FABRICATION: Hodgetts + Fung

ZIP CHIP TECHNOLOGY
San Francisco, 1987
CLIENT: Zip Chip Technology
DESIGN TEAM: John Trautmann, Rachel Vert
INSTALLATION: Systems 32
FABRICATION: Hodgetts + Fung

Film Production/Special Effects

CADILLAC EL DORADO COMMERCIAL
Hollywood, California, 1985
CLIENT: Filmfair Incorporated

COCA COLA COMMERCIAL
Hollywood, California, 1985
CLIENT: Filmfair Incorporated

NIGHTFALL
Arcosanti, New Mexico, 1985
CLIENT: New Horizon Production

STARMAN
1985
CLIENT: Michael Douglas Productions

WANG COMMERCIAL
1985
CLIENT: Robert Abel & Associates

ROCK AND ROLL HOTEL
Richmond, Virginia, 1984
CLIENT: Sweet Production

ECOTOPIA, conceptual design
1982
CLIENT: The Blum Group

Industrial Design/Furniture

WIRE FRAME MODULAR DISPLAY SYSTEM
1994
Giorgio Beverly Hills

AIRFRAME ALUMINUM FURNITURE
1990
Gallery of Functional Art, Los Angeles

HEMDALE OFFICE FURNITURE SYSTEM
1990
Hemdale Film Corporation, Los Angeles

MICROSHOP: INTERACTIVE KIOSK
1986
Intertac Corporation, Los Angeles

HEAVEN PLAYTHINGS
1975
Design Research, New York

NEMO
1975
Design Research, New York

PUNCH-OUT CARDBOARD FURNITURE
1974
Design Research, New York / Yoshichu Corporation,
Japan
DESIGN TEAM: Peter de Bretteville, Keith Godard,
Arthur Golding

LINC HOUSING SYSTEM (prototype)
1969
DESIGN PARTNERS: Keith Godard, Lester Walker

Exhibitions/Installations

CRAIG HODGETTS

"Excavations," PS1, New York, 1981

"Ecotopian Suite," Gallerie Phillip Bonnafont,
San Francisco, 1980

"Work from Studio Works," Mayne Gallery,
Venice, California, 1979

"Architectural Views: Physical Fact Psychic Effect,"
Los Angeles Institute of Contemporary Art, 1978

"Inside James Stirling," Walker Art Center,
Minneapolis, 1977

"The River: Images of the Mississipi,"
Walker Art Center, Minneapolis, 1977

"VIII Venice Biennale," Venice, Italy, 1976

"Works," University of Houston, School of Architecture,
1976

"Low Rise High Density," Museum of Modern Art,
New York, 1974

CRAIG HODGETTS AND HSIN-MING FUNG

"La Città Pulpa," Milan Triennale, Milan, Italy, 1996

"Beyond Architecture: Drawings, Sketches & Other
Media," University of California at Los Angeles, 1995

"Hodgetts + Fung: Selected Works & Drawings," 3A
Garage, San Francisco, 1995

"Reflections of Working Women: Building the Public
Environment," Los Angeles City Hall, Los Angeles, 1993

"Angels & Franciscans: Innovative Architecture from
Los Angeles and San Francisco," Leo Castelli/Gagosian
Gallery, New York, 1992; Santa Monica Museum of Art,
Santa Monica, California, 1993

"Centripetal Vision," American Academy in Rome, Italy,
1992

"Five Shrines," World Financial Center, New York, 1992

"Conceptual Drawings by Architects," Bryce Bannatyne
Gallery, Los Angeles, 1991

Skinner's Room, "Visionary San Francisco," San
Francisco Museum of Modern Art, 1991

"Airframe," Gallery of Functional Art, Los Angeles,
1990

"Arts Park L.A.," Artspace Gallery, Woodland Hills,
California, 1989

"Franklin/La Brea Low Income Housing," The Museum
of Contemporary Art, Los Angeles, 1989

"ADPSR," Max Protetch Gallery, New York, 1988

"The Experimental Tradition: Twenty-Five Years of
American Architecture Competitions, 1960-1986,"
National Academy of Design, New York; High Museum,
Atlanta; National Building Museum, Washington, DC;
University of Minnesota Art Museum, Minneapolis;
University of Quebec, Montreal; Ft. Wayne Museum of
Art, Texas, 1988

"L.A. 12 + 12," Pacific Design Center, Los Angeles, 1988

"The New Urban Landscape," World Financial Center,
Battery Park City, New York, 1988

"Buenos Aires Architecture Biennial," National
Museum of Fine Arts, Buenos Aires, Argentina, 1987

"The Emerging Generation in the USA," GA Gallery,
Tokyo, Japan, 1987

"Small Works," University of California at Los Angeles,
1986

"84 L.A. Architects," Museum of Science and Industry,
Los Angeles, 1984

Awards

1996
Chrysler Award for Innovation in Design,
Chrysler Corporation,
Best of Category, Environments
I.D.: The International Design Magazine, 42nd Annual
Design Review, "Sun Power: No More Daisy"

1994
Architecture Award, American Academy of Arts and
Letters
The I.D. Forty, *I.D.: The International Design Magazine*

1993
Award of Excellence, AIA/American Library
Association, Towell Library
Merit Award, AIA/California Chapter, Towell Library
International Illumination Design, Towell Library
Merit Award, AIA/Los Angeles Chapter, Viso House
Honoree, "L.A. Winners," Architectural Foundation of
Los Angeles

1992
Creative Business Award, Click & Flick Agency

1990
Interior Award, *Architectural Record*, Hemdale Film
Corporation and Office Facility
Special Commendation, AIA/Los Angeles Chapter,
"Blueprints for Modern Living:History and Legacy of
the Case Study Houses"

1989
First Award, The Cultural Foundation, Los Angeles
Arts Park

1987
Meritorious Award, West Hollywood Civic Center
competition

1985
Excellent Entry, Seoul Summer Olympics Athletes'
and Reporters' Village

1984
First Design Award, *Progressive Architecture*,
Cookie Express
First Award, Little Tokyo Design Competition

1982
First Design Award, *Progressive Architecture*,
Southside Settlement Community Center

1976
First Design Award, *Progressive Architecture*,
Venice Interarts Center

1972
First Design Award, *Progressive Architecture*,
Southside Settlement Community Center
First Design Award, *Progressive Architecture*,
00:00, A Mobile Theater

1969
First Design Award, *Progressive Architecture*,
Decitrun 636 Building

Select Bibliography

ARTICLES ON HODGETTS + FUNG

"Frank O. Gehry: EMR Communication and Technology Center," *GA Document* 45 (December 1995): 30-47 ("Sun Power" exhibit design).

Schmidt-Lorenz, Klaus. "Ökologische Dekonstruktion," *Design Report*, November 1995, pp. 64-67.

Hyatt, Peter. "Advanced Learning Curves," *Steel Profile*, September 1995, pp. 18-25.

Gregory, Daniel. "Stylish isles," *Sunset*, April 1995, p. 140.

Borghi, Ruggero. "Verde giallo viola," *Ville Giardini*, March 1995, pp. 10-14.

Bussel, Abby. "The (Social) Art of Architecture," *Progressive Architecture*, January 1995, pp. 43-46.

Jodidio, Philip. "Architects Californiens," *Connaissance des Arts*, October 1994, pp. 100-139.

Antonelli, Paola. "Economy of Thought, Economy of Design," *Abitare*, May 1994, pp. 243-249.

Irace, Fulvio. "The Building of an Architectural Identity," *Abitare*, May 1994, pp. 212-217.

Drewes, Frank F. "Bibliothek UCLA in Los Angeles, USA," *Deutsche Bauzeitschrift*, April 1994, pp. 49-54.

Milshtein, Amy. "Hot Towell," *Contract Design*, March 1994, pp. 60-63.

Betsky, Aaron. "The I.D. Forty: Contemporary Solutions," *I.D.: The International Design Magazine*, January-February 1994, p. 49.

Renger, Reinhard. "Regie Für Bunte Würfel," *Ambiente*, January-February 1994, pp. 96-101.

Leclerc, David. "Bibliothèque provisoire Towell," *L'Architecture d'Aujourd'hui*, December 1993, pp. 92-95.

Betsky, Aaron. "Casting Castle," *Architectural Record*, October 1993, pp. 92-95.

Muschamp, Herbert. "A Bright Balloon of a Building Soars at U.C.L.A.," *New York Times*, Aug. 8, 1993, p. 29.

Bussel, Abby. "Now You See It," *Progressive Architecture*, June 1993, pp. 104-107.

Lamprecht, Barbara. "Bibliotheca Temporaria," *The Architectural Review*, June 1993, pp. 38-43.

Forster, Kurt W. "Panem et Circenses," *a+u*, May 1993, pp. 28-31.

Pröhl, Undine. "Das Ende Steht Nahe Bevor," *Hauser*, May 1993, pp. 82-85.

"Hodgetts and Fung," *a+u*, May 1993, pp. 10-27.

Betsky, Aaron. "Under the Big Top," *Architectural Record*, March 1993, pp. 94-101.

————. "Biggest Show on Earth," *I.D.: The International Design Magazine*, January/February 1993, p. 24.

Puzy, Dennis. "House of Many Colors," *House and Garden*, September 1992, pp. 94-97.

Mays, Vernon. "Carving a Niche for the '90s: Entertainment Design," *Architecture*, May 1992, pp. 96-97.

Webb, Michael. "Hollywood Blockbuster," *Belle Design and Decoration*, February-March 1992, pp. 60-67.

Garcia-Marques, Francesca. "Arts Park, Los Angeles," *L'ARCA*, September 1991, pp. 40-45.

Rasch, Horst. "Paradis Vogel à la Hollywood," *Hauser*, May 1991, pp. 24-31.

Betsky, Aaron. "The New Colors of Modernism," *Metropolitan Home*, April 1991, pp. 150-155.

Forster, Kurt W. "Beauty (and the beast) in the Parlor: Hodgetts + Fung's Architecture in the (C)Age of Media Culture," *a+u*, March 1991, pp. 68-128.

Lyndon, Donlyn, and Neema Kudva. "Visionary San Francisco: Portfolio/ Visions of Movement: Exhibition Notes," *Places: A Quarterly Journal of Exhibition Design* 7, no. 2 (Winter 1991): 21-33.

Polledri, Paolo. " Visionary San Francisco: Dreamscape, Reality and Afterthoughts," *Places: A Quarterly Journal of Environmental Design* 7, no. 2 (Winter 1991): 8-20.

Muschamp, Herbert. "Craig Hodgetts, Ming Fung: You Send Me," *Terrazzo* 4 (1990): 93–108.

Webb, Michael. "Aloft in the Hollywood Hills," *L.A. Style*, November 1990, pp. 184–187.

Arcidi, Philip. "Projects," *Progressive Architecture*, September 1990, pp. 143–146.

Betsky, Aaron. "Change in Scene," *Architectural Record*, September 1990, pp. 104–109.

Scott, Nancy. "San Francisco Future(s): Visions and Revisions," *Metropolitan Home*, July 1990, p. 32.

"New Case Study Housing: MOCA Housing Competition, Franklin/La Brea, Hollywood, 1988," *GA Houses* 29 (July 1990): 16–21.

Gallagher, Larry. "Brave New City," *S.F. Magazine*, June 1990, pp. 70–77.

"Hodgetts and Fung Design Associates: Viso Residence and Thames Residence," *GA Houses* 28 (March 1990): 96–99.

Suisman, Douglas R. "Utopia in the Suburbs," *Art in America*, March 1990, pp. 184–193.

Smith, Elizabeth A. T. "Introduction," *Blueprints for Modern Living: History and Legacy of the Case Study Houses* (Los Angeles: Museum of Contemporary Art; and Cambridge, Mass., and London: MIT Press, 1989).

Antonelli, Paola. "Storia ed Eredità Delle Case Study Houses," *Domus*, December 1989, pp. 10–11.

McCoy, Esther. "Perspectives: Case Study Houses Remembered at MOCA," *Progressive Architecture*, December 1989, pp. 33–34.

Betsky, Aaron. "Steel Chic and Stucco Dreams: At the L.A. Lab," *Metropolitan Home*, August 1989, pp. 75–87.

"Beautification Takes Command," *Bauwelt* 80, no. 16/17 (April 1989): 770–771.

Whiteson, Leon. "P/A Portfolio: Housing for the Future," *Progressive Architecture*, October 1988, p. 96.

White, Garrett. "Sci-Arc: Revolutionary Architecture," *L.A. Style*, September 1988, pp. 166–175, 264.

Holt, Steven, and Michael McDonough. "Apocalypse Now: The New L.A.," *Metropolitan Home*, July 1988, p. 24.

Holt, Steven. "Creative Trends, World Pulse, New York," *Axis*, vol. 28 (Summer 1988): 23.

Viladas, Pilar, and Susan Doubilet. "UC Builds," *Progressive Architecture*, May 1988, pp. 85–93.

Betsky, Aaron. "The Ephemerality of a Cinema Architecture," *Architectural Review*, December 1987, pp. 59–60.

————. "Villa Linda Flora, The Emerging Generation, USA," *GA Houses Special* 2 (November 1987): 22–27.

"Cookie Express: Architectural Design Citation," *Progressive Architecture*, January 1985, pp. 124–125.

"International Architecture Competition for '88 Seoul Olympic Athletes' & Reporters' Village," *Magazine for Architectural Culture* (Korea), July 1985, pp. 30–59.

BOOKS ON HODGETTS + FUNG

Jodidio, Philip. *Contemporary California Architects* (Cologne, Germany: Benedikt Taschen Verlag, 1995).

Lacy, Bill, and Susan deMenil. *Angels & Franciscans: Innovative Architecture from Los Angeles and San Francisco* (New York: Rizzoli International Publications, 1992).

Martin, Richard, ed. *The New Urban Landscape*. Exhibition catalogue (New York: Olympia & York Companies, Drenttel Doyle Partners, and Rizzoli International Publications, 1990).

Polledri, Paolo. *Visionary San Francisco* (Munich: Prestel-Verlag, 1990).

Langdon, Philip. *Orange Roofs, Golden Arches* (New York: Alfred A. Knopf, 1986).

Giovannini, Joseph. *Real Estate as Art: New Architecture in Venice, California.* (Venice, Calif.: Sewell Archives, 1984).

California Counterpoint: New West Coast Architecture 1982. Exhibition catalogue (New York: Institute for Architecture and Urban Studies, 1982).

Forster, Kurt. *New West Coast Architecture* (New York: Rizzoli International Publications, 1982).

Lesser, Massimo. *American Architectural Alternatives: London, Paris, Amsterdam, Zurich, Rome, and Madrid, 1979-80: The Second Western Alternative*. Exhibition catalogue. n.p., 1980.

Drexler, Arthur, curator. *Another Chance for Housing: Low-Rise Alternatives*. Exhibition catalogue (New York: The Museum of Modern Art, 1973).

ARTICLES ON STUDIO WORKS

"Architectural Design Citation: Robert Mangurian and Craig Hodgetts Studio Works," *Progressive Architecture*, January 1983, pp. 90-91.

Jencks, Charles. "Hodgetts and Mangurian," *Free-Style Classicism: Architectural Design Profile 52*, no. 1/2 (London: Architectural Design, 1982): 54-57.

"Building of the Quarter: Palazzo Gagosian," *Archetype* 2, no. 4 (Fall 1982): 14-19.

"A Palazzo in Venice," *Wet Magazine*, March/April 1981, pp. 43-49.

Goldstein, Barbara. "Gagosian Studio: Venetian Masque," *Progressive Architecture*, February 1981, pp. 86-89.

Mack, Mark. "Southside Settlement: Memory Materialized," *Progressive Architecture*, February 1981, pp. 70-05.

Giovannini, Joseph. "California Design: New West Side Story," *Interiors*, December 1980, pp. 50-51, 80-82.

Boissiere, Olivier. "Ten California Architects: Craig Hodgetts/Robert Mangurian," *Domus*, March 1980, pp. 17-20.

"Mississippi The River: Project for Minneapolis," *Domus*, March 1977, pp. 26-30.

"The 24th Awards Program," *Progressive Architecture*, January 1977, pp. 47-65.

Stern, Robert A. M. "Some Notes on the New 'Forty under Forty,'" *a+u*, January 1977, pp. 104-105.

"Suburban Alternatives: Eleven American Projects," *Biennale di Venezia/ VIII Venice Biennale*, vol. 2, general catalogue (Venice: Biennale di Venezia, 1976), p. 258.

Friedman, Mildred S. "The River: Images of the Mississippi/Nicollet Island: A New View," *Design Quarterly* 101/102 (1976): 74-75.

"Studio Works, Southside Settlement: First Design Award," *Progressive Architecture*, January 1976, pp. 62-63.

"Prototipi/Prototypes: Nemo and Heaven," *Domus*, June 1975, pp. 39-40.

"Cari Bambini/Dear Tots," *Abitare*, September 1974, p. 39.

Moore, Eudorah M. "Designs to Satisfy Today's Needs," *Design U.S.A.* (Los Angeles: Broadway Department Stores & California Design Department of the Pasadena Art Museum, 1972), pp. 30-37.

"00:00, A Mobile Theater: First Design Award," *Progressive Architecture*, January 1972, pp. 94-98.

"A View of Contemporary World Architecture, *Japan Architect* 45, no. 7 (July 1970): 87.

Okada, Shin'ichi; Nobutaka Ashihara; and Toshio Yamamoto. "A View of Contemporary World Architecture," *Japan Architect*, July 1970, pp. 81-87.

"Technology and Image: First Design Award, Decitrun CJC Building," *Progressive Architecture*, January 1969, pp. 140-146.

"Lowering the Cost of Housing," *Progressive Architecture*, June 1968, pp. 94-107.

Rosenblatt, Arthur. "The New Visionaries: Yale Graduate School Project for MAXX Housing," *Metropolitan Museum of Art Bulletin*, April 1968, p. 327.

ESSAYS AND ARTICLES BY CRAIG HODGETTS

"Requiem for a Heavyweight," *Blueprint*, December/January 1995, pp. 59-63.

"Engineering Dystopia: Hard Solutions to Soft Problems," *Architecture California* 16:2 (November 1994): 75.

"Rubbing Out the Craft: Architecture and Fabrication in the Age of Information," *Architecture California* 16:1 (May 1994): 7-11.

"Heretical Remarks on Architecture and Photography," *Architecture California* 14:1 (May 1992): 57-63.

"Behind the Action: Architecture and the Vision of Reason in the Age of MTV," *Design Book Review* 24 (Spring 1992): 12-15.

"Book Review: Eames Design," *Annals of the Architecture Association* 20 (Autumn 1990): 108-109.

"Swimming to Suburbia," *Los Angeles Forum* (1989): 48.

"All the Ideas," *Occluded Front: James Turrell* (Larkspur Landing, CA: The Lapis Press, 1985).

"Inside James Stirling," *Design Quarterly* 100 (1977): 84.

"Dragging the Brion-Vega and Other Stories," *Progressive Architecture*, November 1973, pp. 77-80.

"Biography of a Teaching Machine," *Artforum*, February 1973, pp. 61-65.

"Architecture for the Liberated Community," *Ms. Magazine*, January 1972, pp. 122-127.

"The Synthetic Landscape," *Arts in Society*, Fall 1970, pp. 126-132.

"Conceptual Architecture," *Design Quarterly*, Spring 1970, pp 76-77.

"Polis '76: A proposal for the 1976 World's Fair," *New York Magazine*, June 24, 1970 (collaboration with Robert Mangurian).

"LINC Housing System," *L'Architecture d'Aujourd'hui*, February-March 1970, pp. 63-67 (collaboration with Keith Godard, Lester Walker).

"The Boys Walk this Way, the Girls Walk that Way," *West Magazine*, January 12, 1970 (collaboration with Peter de Bretteville).

"UniverCity Now," *Glamour*, August 1969, pp. 161-165 (collaboration with Keith Godard, Lester Walker).

"Redesigning New York: An Immodest Proposal," *New York Magazine*, February 24, 1969, pp. 33-43 (collaboration with Lester Walker).

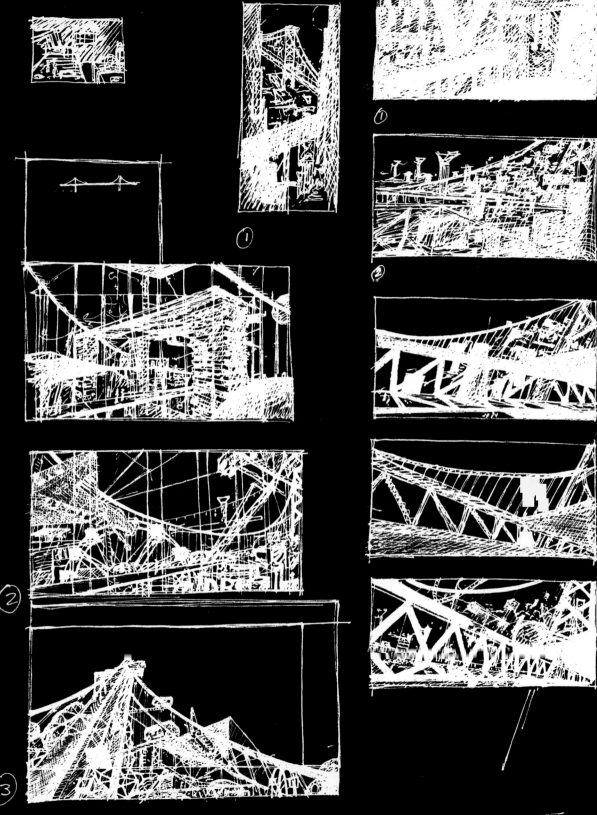

USF
MARCH 24 '90

Biographies

CRAIG HODGETTS

Born, 1937

1955-1957
General Motors Institute, Flint, MI
1957-1960
Oberlin College, Oberlin, OH, Bachelor of Arts,
Fine Arts
1961-1962
San Francisco State University
1962-1964
University of California at Berkeley
1964-1966
Yale University, School of Art and Architecture,
Master of Architecture
1967
Conklin and Rossant, Architects, New York
1967-1968
James Stirling, Architect, New York
1968-1983
Studio Works, Principal and Co-Founder, New York
and Venice, CA
1984-present
Hodgetts+Fung Design Associates, Principal
and Co-Founder, Santa Monica, CA
1989-present
Harmonica, Inc., Principal and Co-Founder,
Santa Monica, CA

PROFESSIONAL AFFILIATIONS

1995
International Design Conference, Aspen, CO,
invited speaker
1992
American Academy in Rome, selection jury
1990
Vietnam Women's War Memorial, competition jury
1987
AIA/San Diego Chapter, Honor Awards jury
NEA Design Advancement Panel
1986
AIA/Los Angeles Chapter, competition jury
AIA Minnesota Society, Honor Awards jury
NEA Design Advancement Panel
NEA USA Fellowship, Policy Panel
Pershing Square (Los Angeles), competition jury

1985
Architectural League of New York, competition jury
MOCA Primary Education Task Force (Los Angeles)
NEA Design Advancement Panel
NEA Panel on Architect/Artist Collaborations
1984
Escondido Civic Center (California), competition jury
Domaine Clos Pegase, competition jury
1977
Progressive Architecture Design Awards, jury
1975
California Council on Design Education
Task Force Federal Design Assembly
Task Force Second Federal Design Assembly,
Program Committee

ACADEMIC AFFILIATIONS

1993-present
Professor, University of California at Los Angeles,
Graduate School of Art and Architecture
1995
Eero Saarinen Visiting Professor Chair of Architectural
Design, Yale University, School of Architecture
1990-1993
Professor, University of California at San Diego,
Graduate School of Architecture
1982-1990
Adjunct Professor, University of Pennsylvania, Graduate
School of Fine Arts
1984
Visiting Professor, Rice University
1969-1972
Associate Dean, California Institute of the Arts,
School of Design

HSIN-MING FUNG

Born, 1953

1971-1973
Oxford College, Oxford, OH
1973-1974
Miami University, Oxford, OH
1975-1977
California State University, Dominguez Hills,
Bachelor of Arts, Behavioral Sciences
1977-1980
University of California at Los Angeles,
Master of Architecture
1980-1984
Charles Kober & Associates, Designer
1984-present
Hodgetts+Fung Design Associates, Principal
and Co-Founder, Santa Monica, CA
1989-present
Harmonica, Inc., Principal and Co-Founder,
Santa Monica, CA

PROFESSIONAL AFFILIATIONS

1995-1996
American Adademy in Rome, Rome Prize competition,
jury
1995
International Design Conference, Aspen, CO, Fellow
Los Angeles Forum for Architecture and Urban Design,
President
AIA Iowa, jury
1994-present
Los Angeles Forum for Architecture and Urban Design,
President
Association of Collegiate Schools of Architecture,
Design Projects Review, Chair
1994
The Texas Society of Architects Design Awards, jury
Laguna Beach Architectural Guild 4th Annual Design
Competition, jury
1992-present
The Museum of Contemporary Art, Los Angeles,
Architecture and Design Council, board member
1991-1993
Los Angeles Forum for Architecture and Urban Design,
board member
1990
Vietnam Women's War Memorial, competition jury
1989
Association of Collegiate Schools of Architecture,
Design Projects Review

ACADEMIC AFFILIATIONS

1995
Eero Saarinen Visiting Professor Chair of Architectural
Design, Yale University, School of Architecture
1985-present
California State Polytechnic University, Pomona,
College of Environmental Design, Department of
Architecture
    1990-1996, Associate Professor
    1986-1990, Assistant Professor
    1985-1986, Lecturer
1993-present
Visiting Professor, Southern California Institute of
Architecture

PHOTOGRAPHY CREDITS

All photographs and images except those noted below courtesy of
Hodgetts + Fung Design Associates. Numbers refer to page numbers.

© Jay L. Ahrend: 53

© Artog: 26 (center), 34, 36 (top)

© Tom Bonner: 94, 100 (top), 106 (top), 107 (top left), 114, 118, 119 (top), 123

© Angela Fisher: 60 (top right, center right)

© Craig Hodgetts: 20, 21, 22-23, 27 (top), 29 (top left and right), 31 (top), 32 (top right), 33 (top), 37 (top), 47 (bottom left and right), 60 (bottom center and right), 131, 139, 141, 143 (bottom left), 145 (top), 146

© L.A. Aerial Photography: 130

© Cam de Leon: 93 (bottom, drawing)

© Robert Mangurian: 18, 26 (top left), 33 (bottom right), 35

© Grant Mudford: 2-3, 137, 144 (top right), 145 (top), 150-51

© Ken Naverson: 144 (top), 147 (top)

© Jayme Odgers: 28 (bottom), 29 (bottom left and right), 143 (bottom left and right)

© Marvin Rand: 78, 81, 83, 87 (top), 90 (top), 91, 92 (top), 93 (top), 108 (bottom left and center)

© Schindler Archive: 47 (center)

© Julius Shulman: 79, 80

© Tim Street-Porter: pp. 30 (bottom left and right), 31 (bottom left)

© Wadsworth Atheneum, Hartford. The Ella Gallup Sumner and Mary Catlin Sumner Collection Fund: 14